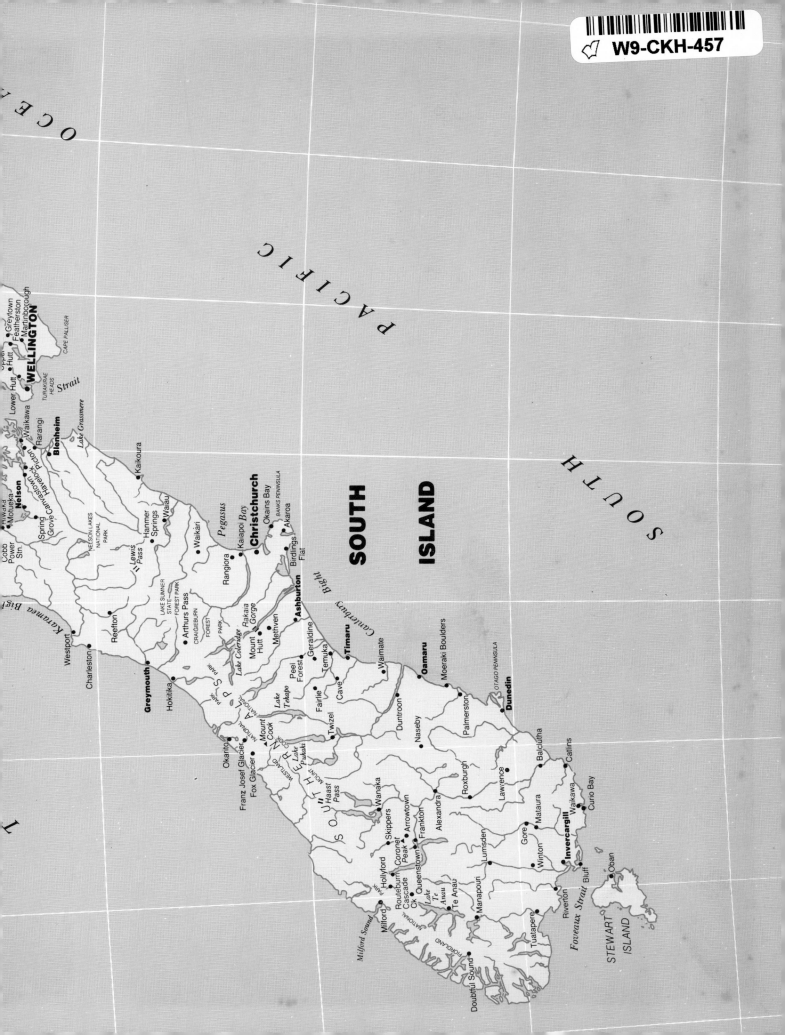

PRESENTING
NEW ZEALAND

PRESENTING NEW ZEALAND

Text by Dalys Conlon

**Photographs by Dawn Kendall, Russell Waite,
Harold Collinson, Ruud Kleinpaste, Steven McIvor,
Fritz Prenzl, Doug Newman, Sue Robinson
and Anna Fairlie**

GOLDEN PRESS

Auckland · Sydney

First edition 1982
Reprinted 1986

Devised and produced by
Child & Henry Publishing Pty Ltd
in association with Dalys Conlon Publishing

Published by
Golden Press Pty Ltd
717 Rosebank Road, Avondale, Auckland, and
35 Osborne Street, Christchurch, New Zealand

ISBN 0 85558 758 X

Printed by
Colourwork Press Pte Ltd,
21 Mandai Estate, Singapore

Contents

White Terrace (Tarawera)

1

New Zealand — Land of Contrast

The recreation grounds, New Plymouth

New Zealand — land of the long white cloud — is one of the last outposts in our highly industrialised world. A compact haven of nature's wonders, both residents and tourists marvel at the beauty of this verdant oasis in the Pacific. It is also a land of contrast. The 269 057 square kilometres of countryside contain towering snow-capped peaks, ribbons of glaciers, boiling mud pools, geysers, sheep-studded green pastures and forests of native bush.

Lakes reflect lofty mountain tops and sprawling networks of rivers dissect the plains. More than three-quarters of the over three million New Zealanders live in the cities, but still the presence of mountains and sea dominates their lives. Although the country stretches 1600 kilometres from Cape Reinga in the north to the steep-sided indentations of Fiordland in the south it is not possible anywhere in New Zealand to be more than 110 kilometres from the sea. And along most of this length runs a backbone of mountain ranges.

New Zealanders love their land — it has a freshness and beauty containing the promise of peace and plenty.

The land

Although small in area (1600 kilometres long and a total area of 269 057 square kilometres) the physical landscape of New Zealand is immense in its variety. Its geological history has been turbulent. About one hundred and fifty million years ago New Zealand was probably part of a supercontinent, thought to include South America, Africa, India, Antarctica and Australia, which was later given the name Gondwanaland by a nineteenth-century geologist. Awesome forces moulded this large land mass, fracturing the earth's crust and eventually causing the division of the continent into the land masses they are today. Even when separated from other land masses New Zealand continued to be geologically volatile. Part of the land rose from the sea and volcanoes, earthquakes, glacial movement and erosion combined to form the extremely varied landscape of New Zealand. The forces that build mountains are still active — geological evidence shows that the Southern Alps have been raised one hundred metres in the last ten thousand years.

The basic structural features of New Zealand are vividly reflected by the surface we see today. One of the major wrinkles in the earth's crust formed the entire northern peninsula of the North Island. The second main wrinkle can be seen in the mountain range that runs south from East Cape right down to the Southern Alps in the South Island.

Where these two wrinkles converged, around the centre of the North Island, they caused massive stresses and strains which produced a variety of arresting features in the area known as the volcanic plateau. For two million years great eruptions in this area have altered the landscape for hundreds of square kilometres around.

One particularly violent early eruption occurred about A.D. 135 when a huge bubble of gas and molten rock forced its way out of the earth's surface and created a crater that is now the largest lake in the country — Lake Taupo. Some of the volcanoes in this area are still active. Ngauruhoe, two and a half thousand years old, usually emits a plume of smoke, showing that a safety valve is open. Every few years it spectacularly erupts ash and gas for a short time. The most recent eruption when lava flowed was in 1954 when explosions scattered ash and blocks of lava over the surrounding district. Mt Ruapehu is the highest mountain in the North Island and is still in a very active state. The broad summit has at least two craters, one of which is active and contains a steaming lake.

White Island in the Bay of Plenty is the most continuously active of New Zealand's volcanoes and is often obscured by clouds of steam. Over thirty steam and ash eruptions have been recorded here since 1826. Maori legend attributes the existence of White Island to the hero Maui. After fishing the North Island out of the sea Maui accidentally picked up some of the fire burning on it and threw it back into the sea where it remains today as White Island.

The last major eruption to claim human life in New Zealand was that of Mt Tarawera in 1886. In four hours a roaring eruption transformed most of the surrounding countryside, destroying three settlements and killing more than one hundred people. It was the most violent eruption since European settlement in New Zealand began.

The other manifestation of the volcanic activity in this volatile area is the thermal wonders of the Rotorua district. Boiling mud, hot springs, gushing geysers and a chain of beautiful lakes all attest to the area's long and turbulent geological past. North of the volcanic plateau there is still more evidence of this explosive past. Mt Egmont, quiet now, last erupted two hundred years ago and more than fifty volcanoes dot the metropolitan Auckland area.

To the south and east of the volcanic plateau other physical processes have formed deeply eroded country of steep valleys and tangled ridges. The thrusting headlands that reach out into Cook Strait illustrate the presence of another 'shaky' structural feature: that of fault lines. Some faults are still active, producing the occasional earthquake; the last serious one was in Napier in 1931 when much of the town was destroyed. These fault lines continue across Cook Strait in the form of the huge ranges that run from the Kaikouras into the Southern Alps.

The South Island compared to the North Island is volcanically immobile; the volcanoes that formed Banks and Otago peninsulas are long dead. However, this island has perhaps the most outstanding feature of New Zealand's topography: the 640-kilometre-long mountain ranges of the Southern Alps, the largest and loftiest mountain block of New Zealand. The Alps dominate the landscape and people's impression of it. One early colonist, Laurence Kennaway, wrote these words in 1874:

We lay — for we were too exhausted to stand, upon the highest peak of a great spur or branch of mountain which led, without break, up to the Mt Cook range itself. We could see old Mount Cook (only a church tower lower than Mount Blanc) in the very heart of the Southern Alps, lifting his cragged, storm-beaten head thirteen thousand feet into the air — as the bird flies, not ten miles from us — his steep, glaciered sides sending back the sunlight with a dead white light, such as one sees from ground glass. I am quite hopeless at giving any idea of the frightful mass of mountainous chaos which lay between us and it, and for miles, as far as we could see, towards the western coast of

The glacier system of Mt Cook

the middle island .... It would be impossible to conceive a more life-forgotten place — a jumbled mass of mountain hurled into every chaotic shape and position.

The mountains rise to over 3000 metres in the Mt Cook area and have an average height of 1500 metres. Moulded by one of the world's most distinctive faults, the Alpine Fault, they run straight and uninterrupted from Milford Sound in Fiordland to north of Lewis Pass in Nelson. This great uplift of the earth gave New Zealand some of its most striking scenery.

In late Tertiary times glaciers formed and moved down the eastern and western sides of the mountains. Retreating remnants of glaciers still exist today. These glaciers shaped the grooved alpine valleys forming long finger lakes — some over 80 kilometres long. In the fiords and glaciated valleys of Fiordland and north-west Nelson, clear remains of Ice Age features can be seen and it is not difficult to visualise the glaciers that occupied the breathtaking valleys over twenty thousand years ago.

Post-glacial meltwaters and the rivers have also had a part to play in the creation of the unique South Island scenery. Rivers have carried shingle off the mountains to build up the South Island lowlands, including the impressive Canterbury Plain.

From the sub-tropical north of New Zealand to the rugged and isolated southernmost tip, the regions of the country all offer varied scenic splendour. The North Island's scenery is not as spectacular as the South Island but it does have its appeal. Northland is characterised by land meeting sea, most dramatically so in the Bay of Islands where drowned hills form nearly one hundred and fifty islands. Captain Cook said this area was blessed with 'every kinds of refreshments' and today the pohutukawa-festooned islands and stretches of golden sand lure tourists from all parts of the country. In the far north the sea is seldom more than a kilometre away. Here, the unspoilt beauty of the beaches, towering sand dunes and quiet lonely coves offer stark contrast to the resorts of the Bay of Islands. Northland is also home of the kauri forest. Although greatly depleted by man, groves of these giant forest gods still remain. Waipoua Forest is home of 'Tane Mahuta' — god of the

forest — a giant kauri believed to be 1200 years old, with a girth of 14 metres and height of 51 metres.

The commercial city of Auckland is beautified by both the Hauraki Gulf and the rocky headlands of the West Coast. More than one hundred named islands dot the sheltered Hauraki Gulf and provide a mecca for yachtsmen and nature lovers and a sanctuary for wildlife. On the other side of the Auckland isthmus the bush-clad Waitakere Ranges slope down into iron sand beaches and the great breakers of the Tasman Sea.

Coromandel Peninsula with its craggy ranges and pohutukawa-laced beaches is another favourite holiday haunt. Although heavily exploited by man in the nineteenth century when mining and farming meant the milling and burning of bush and forest, dense rainforest still survives and many rare creatures such as the kokako find sanctuary in isolated forest pockets. High in the ranges, ancient volcanic plugs tower above trees and bush.

The Rotorua area is the most famous of the North Island's tourist attractions. The most important thermal areas here are Whakarewarewa on the edge of Rotorua city, Waimangu, Waiotapu, Tikitere and Orakei Korako. Geysers, boiling mud, hot springs and formations of extraordinary shapes and phosphorescent colours have drawn visitors from the beginnings of commercial tourism about one hundred years ago. These wonders are enhanced by the natural beauties of the region — the chain of beautiful tranquil lakes and the awe-inspiring volcanic craters of Mt Tarawera. Lake Taupo, New Zealand's biggest lake, is another highlight of the Volcanic Plateau and is best known for its trout, many of which weigh over 3 kilograms. The country's best known trout stream, the Tongariro River weaves its way into Lake Taupo through a delta near Turangi.

Volcano-studded Tongariro National Park is the heart of the North Island. Three active volcanoes — Ngauruhoe, Tongariro and Ruapehu — dominate New Zealand's oldest National Park, formally constituted in 1894. The skifields of Ruapehu, interesting scenic walks, cliffs suitable for climbing, along with the brooding grandeur of the mountains make the

Mt Egmont, from the sea

park a popular year-round recreation area.

Urewera National Park and Egmont National Park are the other major North Island national parks. The Urewera holds the largest area of native forest in the North Island and contains abundant native birdlife. The landscape here is diverse: grassy flats, rocky peaks, a lake filled with trout, and rich and varied forest. Lake Waikaremoana ('lake of rippling water') is regarded as the most beautiful lake in the North Island. Mt Egmont dominates the Egmont National Park. The snowy peaks of this isolated volcanic cone contrast with the verdant forest-covered slopes and attract a multitude of climbers. Cascading waterfalls and cut tracks make this one of the prettiest walking areas in the country.

The remote East Cape region offers the visitor wild mountains, a spectacular coast with golden beaches and an extremely temperate climate. The rugged Raukumara Range in the heart of the East Cape played a large part in isolating the area from early settlement with the result that the region now has a large Maori population — about 27 per cent of the land here is owned by Maoris. White Island, an active volcano off the coast of the Bay of Plenty, emits huge clouds of steam and from time to time sprinkles the mainland with fine dust.

The south-east corner of the North Island presents a combination of sheer cliffs, sandy beaches and sheep-studded hills. Gannets nest on the rocky headland of Cape Kidnappers and many other sea birds are found along the generally unpopulated coast.

Waterfall on the Wanganui

New Zealand's most awe-inspiring scenery is to be found in its glacier-moulded South Island. The interlocking land and water of the Marlborough Sounds, the wild Nelson hinterland and the richness of natural life in the sparsely populated Golden Bay area all form a dramatic introduction to the South Island. Further south is the beautiful Nelson Lakes National Park. Here, high ranges and forested valleys yield bush-fringed lakes. The western boundary of the Southern Alps soars through the area, rising above sub-alpine and rainforest plant life.

The sparsely peopled Kaikoura Coast is backed by two parallel mountain ranges; the Seaward Kaikouras and Inland Kaikouras. Snowy mountains tower above the rock-bound coast and lonely farmsteads huddle at the foot of the crumpled inland ranges. Kaikoura means 'meal of crayfish' and, although depleted by commercialism, spiny crayfish are still caught on Kaikoura's reefs and packed for export.

Arthurs Pass National Park is a mountain wilderness of both dense rainforest and beech forest. Glaciers, earthquakes and avalanches have all played their part in forming this area. Arthurs Pass is the highest highway across the Southern Alps, crossing the main divide at nine hundred and twenty metres. The great Waimakariri River finds its source in this region and winds its way to the sea across the fertile Canterbury Plains. The checkerboard flatness of these plains comes to an abrupt halt when they reach the rugged slopes of Banks Peninsula. Formed by massive twin volcanoes, the peninsula is an area of rocky bays, quiet coves and winding valleys. On its southern side lies Lake Ellesmere, a great expanse of inland water noted for its flounder fishing and black swans.

Inland again is Mt Cook National Park — a spectacular area of soaring peaks bordered by turquoise lakes and the brown grasslands of the Mackenzie Country. Mt Cook, New Zealand's highest mountain, rises over 3000 metres above the floors of the Tasman and Hooker valleys. More than one-third of the Park is covered by permanent snow and the creeping ice of large glaciers, such as the 28-kilometre-long Tasman Glacier. The beautiful glacial lakes Tekapo and Pukaki have an extraordinary pale turquoise colour caused by the 'rock flour' carried into them by glacier meltwater. On the eastern boundary of the Park is the Mackenzie Country, a vast treeless basin covered with brown tussock.

West of the Southern Alps is a narrow coastal strip bordered by the Tasman Sea and a long straight wall of mountains. Swift rivers, vast swamplands, placid lakes, sliding glaciers and primeval rainforest make South Westland an area of great unspoilt beauty. Two of the most famous glaciers in New Zealand lie within this region — the Fox and Franz Josef.

Astride the main divide of the Southern Alps is Mt Aspiring National Park, a rugged region with fine walking tracks. Focal point is the majestic peak of Mt Aspiring. Lake Wanaka and Lake Hawea lie just outside the Park. To the east, the plateau of Central Otago rises 600 metres above the coastal strip and is made up of broad basins and wide gentle rock-studded hills and mountains. New Zealand's largest river, the Clutha, swings through Central Otago. At the height of the gold rushes in the 1860s thousands

Lake Tekapo

Mt Cook and the Hooker Glacier

of miners combed its river banks. Tussock grasslands give the area a beautiful tawny colour and the many deciduous trees provide glowing autumnal colours. The region reaches westwards to the popular tourist centre of Queenstown and the sierra-like range of the Remarkables.

Fiordland, an immense and lonely buttress against the Southern Ocean and Tasman Sea, has been carved by monstrous glaciers. It is the wettest and most isolated part of New Zealand with many areas still unexplored. Milford Sound has the most breath-taking fiord scenery in the country and the Milford Track is known as 'the finest walk in the world'. Across Foveaux Strait is the charming, forested Stewart Island.

The island is clothed in native vegetation and supports an abundance of birdlife.

The beginnings — the legend

In the beginning, Papa (the Earth Mother) and Rangi (the Sky Father) clung together with their children huddled between them. The sky lay upon the earth and all was in perpetual darkness. It was a miserable existence and the sons of Rangi and Papa plotted to drive their father

13

away. After many attempts had failed, Tane Mahuta (god of the forest) placed his shoulders against the earth and his feet upon the sky and gradually managed to thrust his father away. So was night distinguished from day. The rain, dew and mist are the tears of the heart-broken Rangi and Papa who had no desire to be separated.

All the sons but one stayed with their mother. Tawhiri, god of the winds, followed

When peace at last descended Tane fashioned the body of a woman out of soil. She became Hine-hauone (the Earth-formed Maid). She and Tane had a daughter, Hine Titama (the Dawn Maid). Hine Titama eventually bore Tane daughters but when she discovered that her father and her husband were the same she was so overcome by shame that she fled to Te Po, the Underworld, where she became known as

Maori girls bathing

Rangi to the sky and unleashed great storms to attack his brothers on earth. Tane's trees were uprooted by a hurricane; Tangaroa, the fish-god, fled and hid in the ocean depths and Rongo and Haumia, the plant deities, were hidden by their mother. Only Tu, the god of uncreated man, stood firmly upon the earth and withstood his brother's onslaught.

Hinenui-o-te-Po (Great-lady-of-darkness) and remained to gather in the souls of her descendants. The children of Tane increased and multiplied and did not know death until the hero Maui was born.

One of the first men, Maui-tikitiki, was born so prematurely that his mother, thinking him dead, wrapped him in some of her hair and cast

14

him into the sea. The gods intervened and his ancestor, Rangi, the Sky Father, drew him up and nursed him back to life. Maui eventually returned to his mother and four brothers and embarked upon a series of super-human feats including the snaring of the sun, obtaining fire from its guardian entity and turning his brother-in-law into a dog.

One day Maui went fishing with his brothers and persuaded them to sail their canoe far into unknown southern waters before he decided to cast his line. He used a richly carved, paua inlaid lure hook, fashioned from the jawbone of his grandmother, Murirangawhenua, and for bait he hit himself on the nose and smeared blood onto this prodigious hook. The line went far into the depths of the sea until it caught on the porch of a carved house lying on the ocean floor. Maui heaved on the line and chanted the following words:

Why do you bite so stubbornly
there below oh Tonganui?
The power of Rangawhenua's jawbone
    is upon you,
You are coming up, You are conquered
You child of the sea-god Tangaroa.

Eventually his catch, a land-fish, was hauled out of the sea and their canoe lay high and dry. Maui then set off to make an offering to the gods for his good fortune saying to his brothers, 'Be patient until I return. Do not cut up our fish, and do not eat until the god has been propitiated and I have returned.'

But before Maui had time to reach the priests and make his offering the brothers started cutting up the fish. The gods were displeased and made the fish toss and writhe about as it was being cut. And that, according to Maori legend, is why New Zealand is rugged, broken and mountainous.

Maoris today call the North Island Te Ika-a-Maui, the fish of Maui; the South Island is thought to be his canoe and Stewart Island its anchor. Maui's fish hook is Cape Kidnappers in Hawkes Bay.

Maui finally met his match when he had an argument with the goddess of death who insisted that death should be permanent. Maui believed that man should die like the moon, which returns, rejuvenated from the pit. Maui set off to find his ancestress, Hinenui-o-te-Po, saying, 'If I can pass right through her body I shall live and she will be the one to die.' He found the old lady asleep with her legs apart and jagged flints of obsidian and greenstone could be seen set between her thighs. Maui began his task of passing through her body and his head and arms had disappeared when the old lady awoke and clapped her legs together cutting Maui in half.

Maui was the first being to die and because he failed in his task of re-entering the womb of the goddess to emerge again all men are mortal.

The Maori as he was

It is not known exactly when man first made landfall on New Zealand but by A.D. 1000 there is evidence of quite substantial habitation around the coast, the shores of Lake Taupo and even central Otago.

The original settlers of New Zealand were Pacific people. With the expansion of the Asian population, people filtered eastwards across Melanesia. Cultures became isolated and developed independently and by about 3000 years ago the Polynesian culture evolved. The first mariners probably arrived in New Zealand in about the eighth century A.D., and they probably came from the islands of Eastern Polynesia — Tahiti, the Marquesas and Cook Islands. These people were known as the moa-hunters and modern ethnologists call them Archaic Maori.

According to Maori tradition the islands Maui had fished up from the sea were discovered by a Tahitian named Kupe in about A.D. 925. He returned to Hawaiki, the ancestral home of the Maori and gave his people sailing directions to the new land he had discovered. About four centuries later, food shortage and war were ravaging the Society Islands and Polynesians began to migrate. Most modern Maori tribes trace their descent to a number of canoes that traditionally made the great journey to New Zealand in the fourteenth century. Amongst the canoes were Arawa, Tainui, Aotea, Mataatua, Horouta, Tohora, Mahahu, and Kurahaupo. Whether these traditions are

A Maori war canoe

true or false, whether New Zealand was settled accidentally or intentionally by these Polynesians is still a matter of conjecture.

There must have been many separate arrivals in New Zealand over the centuries but it was the very early arrivals who laid the base of Polynesian culture from which the Maori culture evolved.

The period when the moa-hunters flourished has been archaeologically confirmed. Charcoal from an oven on a moa-hunter site has been radio-carbon dated at about A.D. 1150. And the fact that New Zealand's first settlers came from eastern Polynesia has been confirmed by the discovery of a burial ground on the island of Maupiti in the Society Islands which matches the most famous of all moa-hunter sites, the burial ground at the Wairau Bar in Marlborough. These findings suggest that the moa-hunters' society was already quite highly developed, so it can be assumed that the country had been inhabited for at least one thousand years before A.D. 1100.

The moa were huge flightless birds with small heads, blunt beaks and massive short legs. They were grazing animals, equivalent in New Zealand to the kangaroo of Australia and the buffalo of America. The name moa was Polynesian for jungle fowl and obviously the earliest settlers applied this name to the giant bird they saw grazing the countryside. The moa-hunters found this bird easy prey — a factor which led to its extinction. Once the moa became extinct the Maoris turned from hunting to a reliance on agriculture.

Little food — apart from berries and fern root — grew wild and although bird and fish life was abundant, the only mammals available for food were the dog and the rat that the Maoris had brought with them from their homes in Polynesia. The practice of cannibalism probably originated because of this lack of meat. A form of systematic agriculture evolved, based on plants introduced by these early Polynesians. Kumara, taro and yam flourished in New Zealand's cooler conditions and planting, weeding and storing crops occupied much of these peoples' time.

The Maoris — named by the Europeans from the Polynesian words *tangata Maori*, 'ordinary man' — were a tribal race. The tribe was made up of sub-tribes (hapu) and whanua, extended family groups. The tribe and family were basic units of society that determined how the individual lived — whom he married, whom he fought and where he lived. The concept of kinship was paramount and tribal ancestors were worshipped along with the gods. At the head of each tribe was the ariki — chief. This was a hereditary position and the ariki was to a certain extent tapu (sacred), possessing much mana (prestige).

16

A group of Maoris. The Maoris were a tribal race and the concept of kinship was of great importance

Maori communities lived in villages, settlements made up of one or two sub-tribes. They were fully self-sufficient, cultivating land and hunting and fishing within their own boundaries. These settlements were usually adjacent to a fortified hilltop pa to which the community would retreat if threatened by attack. Forts were built in strategic positions with a natural barrier, such as a river or swamp, protecting at least one side. Trenches were dug, earth ramparts constructed and the whole area fenced with palisades. Thatched houses and food storage pits were built inside. War became an important element in Maori life. Fighting was a highly developed art. For men, the courage displayed and mana gained in battle were impor-

described the sleeping house or whare puni:

The houses of these people are better calculated for a cold than a hot climate. They are built low and in the form of an oblong square. The framing is of wood or of small sticks and the sides and covering of thatch made of long grass. The door is generally at one end, and no bigger than to admit of a man to creep in and out; just within the door is the fireplace, and over the door, or on one side, is a small hole to let out the smoke. These houses are twenty feet or thirty feet long, others not above half as long; this depends upon the largeness of the family they are to contain....

A Maori war dance

tant ingredients in initiation. Tribal boundaries were precisely defined and as the population increased so did disputes over territory. Spears, clubs and throwing sticks were the instruments of warfare and the highly trained warrior was a specialist in hand-to-hand fighting.

Community life required several buildings for each family — buildings for sleeping, cooking and storing food. The whole family used the sleeping house which was usually very well built to keep out the cold. The cooking house had open end walls (to let out the smoke), a shallow oven pit and pile of cooking stones. Cook

The carved meeting house was the most intricate building found in any Polynesian culture. They were up to 25 metres long, 7 metres high and 9 metres wide. Whilst being constructed — often by the entire tribe — the meeting house was tapu. The building would often take seven or eight years to complete and during this time if a woman or slave entered before the tapu was lifted, construction work would be abandoned. These buildings were elaborately carved, the carvings being a record of tribal history and legend, depicting revered ancestors. They were a symbol of tribal and community pride.

Religion was another extremely important aspect of this early Maori culture. The minister of religion was the tohunga, who was the tribal scholar trained in the most sacred lore of the whare wananga (house of learning). The tohunga was also entrusted with details of tribal history and possessed powers of communicating with the gods. He conducted a wide variety of rituals and wielded great power. In battle he would pluck the heart out of the first man killed and offer it to the god of war and he would preside over all rituals connected with any important occasions. Perhaps his most important task was the decreeing of tapu (holy or taboo) upon people and property. Tapu emanated from the gods and if it was violated

gods, Atua Maori, were classified into Io, the supreme god; departmental gods, such as the personification of natural phenomena; district gods and inferior beings; demons and evil spirits.

The early Maori way of life was hard. There was ritual cannibalism, the constant threat of war, the possibility of enslavement in defeat, and a short life span of about forty years. The total population cannot have been very large — it has been estimated that there were only about 200 000 Maoris in New Zealand by the time of Cook's visit. In their adaptation to a new country and a new way of life they did, however, develop skills that made them one of the greatest of all Polynesian people.

Maori idol carvers

death or misfortune would come to the transgressor. Burial and cultivation grounds were protected by tapu, etiquette was instilled, affairs regulated between men of different status and the social system preserved. Tapu was the regulator of Maori life.

The Maoris believed in a supreme being, the existence of two spirit worlds and in the existence of evil and the underworld. The native

Carving is probably the best known of all Maori art forms. It was a highly regarded occupation and the working of wood, bone and stone in New Zealand reached heights of intricacy rarely seen elsewhere. The Maoris found an unlimited supply of excellent timber in New Zealand — particularly the totara tree with its straight-grained durable wood that was relatively easy to work with stone tools. Carving

19

was usually done with adzes having greenstone blades; for more intricate work fragments of obsidian or volcanic glass were used. Wood carving was most common on door lintels and canoe prows and the working of stone and bone produced beautiful ornaments such as necklaces, pendants and tikis.

Only a small number of basic motifs occur in the immense variety of objects carved. The most common is the human figure, rendered in either stylistic or realistic versions. Most of the figures have a frontal stance with their hands resting on the body. The only individual characteristics depicted were tattoo markings. The tattoo, or moko, was a feature of Maori art. Men were tattooed primarily on the face; women on the lips and chin. The face tattooing was probably the most elaborate in the world. A straight blade was used and the patterns revealed both positive and negative aspects. Towards the end of the nineteenth century only women were tattooed and darning needles were used. Tattoos were first done when the boy or girl reached puberty, serving the purpose of an extremely painful initiation ritual. Warriors later received further tattoos, usually on the face and buttocks.

The Maori had come to a hostile environment when he set sail from Polynesia and landed on the shores of New Zealand. With courage and dignity he settled the new land utilising the natural features of the country and adapting his culture. Probably the most important feature to evolve was a highly developed creativity; the arts of architecture, weaving, tattooing, stone working, singing and dancing flourished more abundantly than anywhere else in Polynesia.

Wild New Zealand

Long isolation of the New Zealand land mass from Australia prevented land mammals from reaching the country. Two species of bats are the only endemic mammals. This isolation did, however, make New Zealand a sanctuary for the other long-established animal life and an outstanding natural heritage evolved. Lizards, tuatara and native frogs were to be found on the mainland and the seashore attracted whales,

seals and dolphins. But the country was largely without mammals and before the arrival of man birds were the dominant form of life. The Maoris brought the rat and the dog with them but it was not until the European settlers arrived that more mammals were introduced into the country. Deer, hare, rabbits, hedgehogs, stoats, weasels and ferrets were all introduced in the late 1800s.

New Zealand now has 33 species of introduced mammals, over 1000 species of insects, 34 species of birds and 14 species of freshwater fish.

Before these mammals were introduced, animal life might have been sparse but birdlife was prolific, with more than two hundred native species. Several of these birds such as the moa, a giant eagle, a species of crow and a pelican became extinct before the arrival of the European. But the majority of native birds — such as the tui and kokako — have survived. The early European settlers brought their own birds with them — thrushes, blackbirds, sparrows, pigeons, pheasant and quail are prolific.

New Zealand's wildlife is made up of a stunning variety of both introduced and indigenous fauna.

Birds are the best known of all New Zealand wildlife. The absence of mammals in early New Zealand created an environment where several species of fearless, flightless and slow-moving birds could evolve. These ranged from the now

Skeletons of moa and Maori

extinct moa, which grazed on open grasslands, to New Zealand's most famous bird, the kiwi. Found only in New Zealand, this flightless bird's diet was insects, grubs and worms, supplemented by leaves, berries and seeds. Their body is cone-shaped, tapering from heavy, powerful legs to a fairly small head. They have long, slender, down-curved bills with nostrils near the tip; this long sensitive bill is used to probe deep into the soil for worms and grubs. Remnants of wings are concealed behind their shaggy plumage. The Maori named this bird after its shrill, prolonged call 'ki-wi'. Nocturnal in habit, the kiwi lives in burrows in the ground and lays enormous smooth white or greenish white eggs. The egg of the brown kiwi averages one-fifth of the female's weight — a greater proportion than the egg of any other bird.

The takahe, kakapo and weka were other birds who came to rely on the forest floor for their food supply and felt no need to return to the trees above.

The takahe is a large bird standing approximately 50 centimetres with beautifully coloured plumage. Their head, neck, breast and abdomen are a rich blue; back, rump, tail and wing feathers olive green, the under-tail feathers white, and bill and feet red. They are one of the rarest birds in the world and unique to New Zealand. Now an endangered species, they were considered extinct until 1948 when a small population was found in a remote valley near Lake Te Anau. Their present population is estimated to be between two hundred and two hundred and fifty. They are highly territorial birds requiring between 2 and 56 hectares of feeding ground to satisfy their voracious appetites. Both male and female share incubation of the eggs; the normal clutch is two. After 30 days incubation the jet black chick emerges. By the age of one month the chick has acquired his adult plumage and progressed from a diet of insects to that of vegetation. Both male and female are similar in appearance and most of them remain in pairs for life.

The owl-like, ground-dwelling nocturnal parrot, the kakapo, is even rarer than the takahe. Beautifully patterned in greens and yellows with black and brown flecks, the kakapo dwells in the densely forested mountain ranges of the South Island. They prefer the mossy beech forest up to the tree-line and the alpine meadows above. Although flightless, the bird's strong claws and bill enable it to climb well and the wings are only used for balance when running or climbing. Another unusual characteristic of this bird is its strange method of feeding; it chews blades of grass, rolls it into pellets and sucks out the juice, then leaves the grass dangling from the stem, fibrous and desiccated. Until 1977 there were only an estimated 20 kakapos in New Zealand. A new population has been found on Stewart Island but the numbers have yet to be investigated.

The weka, a member of the rail family, can be often found strutting into campsites and stealing food and equipment. A very inquisitive bird, the weka is found in West Coast forest and farmlands. Plumage is usually a chestnut brown and the bird has large strong legs and feet.

Another cheeky bird is the kea, a native parrot. Commonly called the mountain parrot, the kea can be found in the high country of the Southern Alps, Nelson and Marlborough. It is the most mischievous of all New Zealand birds. Trampers and campers are often treated to the exuberant antics of this olive green and scarlet bird — unlacing boots and tents, tearing fabrics and glissading down the iron roofs of mountain huts. It nests either in burrows in the roots of large trees or amongst loose rocks. Although a strong flier, it spends most of its time on the ground foraging for alpine beetles.

More commonly found amongst the birdlife of New Zealand are the wood pigeon, kaka, tui, and bellbird. The most handsome of all the berry eaters is the wood pigeon, with its iridescent green and purple feathers. Although much sought after by the Maori for its delicate flesh and beautiful plumage that was used for cloak decoration, the bird is still widespread and now protected by law. It feeds on the berries of native trees and can often be seen flying in a spectacular low swoop over open countryside.

The kaka, or brown parrot, is similar in size to the wood pigeon. Not as common as the pigeon, greatly reduced numbers of kaka survive in the north Auckland kauri forests and in podocarp forest and bush in the South Island. Kaka feathers, especially the striking red of the underwings, were also much prized by the

Maori. The bird feeds mainly on berries and nectar but also uses its sensitive tongue to tap the bark on trees for insect grubs.

Best known of all New Zealand's winged birds is the tui. Belonging to a predominantly Australian species of honey-eaters, the tui's beautiful liquid song can be heard in both bush and suburban gardens. The tui's plumage is an iridescent blue-green colour, broken only by a prominent white throat tuft.

Bellbirds at the nest

The bellbird is another bird with a beautiful song — a chiming of four flute-like notes sounded in continuous rhythm, described by Cook as like small, exquisitely tuned bells. The song is usually heard at dawn when the air is filled with a melodious chorus. Two-thirds the size of a tui, the bellbird catches the attention of the ear rather than the eye as its greenish hue harmonises well with the bush surroundings. Another honey-eater, the bellbird strays long distances from its breeding grounds to find nectar of kowhai, fuchsia, rata, puriri and pohutukawa.

The shy and attractive kokako belongs to the wattlebird family and although found in isolated pockets it is fast becoming an endangered species. According to Maori legend, the kokako brought the hero Maui a drink when he returned exhausted from a trip to the sun. Maui rewarded the little bird by stretching its legs, thus enabling it to run and climb more nimbly. About the same size as a magpie, the blue-wattled kokako is a blue-grey colour with a striking black band extending across the base of the beak. Kokakos are rarely seen as they nest high up in the forest canopy and are poor fliers.

Swamps and marshland are the domain of the pukeko, a member of the rail family. Seen throughout New Zealand, the deep blue, red-beaked pukeko is a good swimmer and spends most of its time fossicking near water for its diet of snails, worms, insects and plant matter. Although ungainly in flight it can cover long distances.

New Zealand's seabirds usually nest in colonies on offshore islands and on the more inaccessible rocky headlands. Most famous of all these colonies is the gannet colony on Cape Kidnappers, a rugged promontory jutting into the Pacific. This is the only known mainland nesting site of the Australasian gannet. In 1933, Cape Kidnappers became a bird sanctuary and today about 4500 gannets nest in the area. The gannet is one of the best known of New Zealand's seabirds and the large white birds with long, black-tipped wings and strong, pointed, blue-grey beak are often seen executing spectacular fishing dives at sea.

The only native mammals of New Zealand are two species of small bats. The short-tailed bat is unique to New Zealand but the long-tailed bat is a member of a genus that has relatives in Australia. Both species are strictly bush dwellers and may be seen only at twilight as they noiselessly pursue moths and mayflies over clearings, streams and rivers. They capture and chew these insects with sharp teeth which can inflict a painful bite. The short-tailed bats have an unusual method of folding their wings which enable them to be more active on the ground than most other species of bats. The long-tailed bats hibernate in hollow trees or caves during the winter months when flying insects are scarce.

Geckos and tuataras are the main representatives of the reptile family in New Zealand. The unique, nocturnal tuatara is peculiar to New Zealand. Similar to a lizard in appearance, it is the only surviving member of an extinct family, the *Rynchocephalia*, meaning 'beak-headed'. This family lived in other parts of the world one hundred to two hundred million years ago and the tuatara is commonly known as New Zealand's 'living fossil'. Although there is evidence that this creature lived on the mainland during recent times it is now found only on islands off the east coast of the North Island and on a group of islands in the Marlborough Sounds. The type of terrain that they thrive on includes boulder-strewn beaches, patchy scrub and forest floor pock-marked with seabirds' burrows. They feed on beetles, moths, crickets and wetas and often catch small skinks and geckos. The tuatara has a scaly, wrinkly skin and a crested head, neck and back. It inhabits burrows in loose soil or shares the burrows of seabirds such as the petrel. Clutches of eight to fifteen eggs are laid at the bottom of a shallow bed in late spring. The female then covers the hole and ignores it. Fifteen months later the young force their way out and are immediately independent. Sexual maturity is reached after about twenty years. The lifespan of a tuatara is not known but has been estimated to be at least twenty years. They are now rigidly protected by the government.

The gecko, a true lizard, is usually nocturnal and is found in or near the bush or forest. There are three genera in New Zealand: one represented by three species in the North Island; one widespread over both islands and the third comprises six species found in the South Island. The Auckland green tree gecko is the most striking of all North Island geckos. It is a vivid green and the inside of its mouth a deep, brilliant blue. The South Island geckos are diurnal tree dwellers and probably the prettiest of all New Zealand's geckos. Their patterns are made up of exquisite groupings of lines, spots, diamonds and blotches. Geckos generally have loose-fitting skins covered with small scales. The outer layers of skin are shed at intervals, the whole process generally taking about two hours.

There are three species of small native frogs in the country, the presence of which strengthens the likelihood that New Zealand was once part of a larger land mass. The native frogs differ from their introduced relatives in that they have no ear drums or vocal sacs. Due to the lack of vocal sacs these tiny 40-millimetre-long creatures can only emit a very un-froglike squeak. Their other distinctive feature is their eyes which are enormous, protruding above the top of their head like an alligator's. The frogs do not have a tadpole stage — the embryo passes through its metamorphosis within a capsule and emerges as a miniature frog with a tail which is lost after a few weeks. Habitat varies. One very rare species is found in a small area of rock near Stephens Island, another high in the mountains in the Coroman-

del Ranges, and the third near water or damp mossy rocks. It is believed that these frogs were in this country well over one hundred and twenty million years ago.

Insect life in New Zealand is varied and prolific. The largest and best known of the forest insects is the weta. This fearsome looking insect is a relative of the cricket and is found in caves, trees and on the ground. They have huge hind legs which produce a distinctive rasping sound when rubbed against the ridges of the abdomen. Night is usually their feeding time and they are primarily vegetarian, eating wood and leaves. They are very agile and can jump long distances amongst the branches or along the ground. The giant weta is the most spectacular of all the wingless insects. Surviving in only small numbers on Little Barrier Island they reach a length of over 9 centimetres and weigh up to 80 grams — one of the largest insects in the world. The ugliness of the species was reflected by the Maori word for them: wetapunga, punga being the god who ruled over the deformed and ugly creatures. Wetas have a long fossil history dating back to one hundred and ninety million years ago and are representative of a very ancient group of insects that have changed little over the millennia.

One of the very few creatures in New Zealand that is potentially dangerous to man is the katipo spider. Fortunately, it is a shy retiring creature found mainly under driftwood on the foreshore. The fully grown female is the dangerous one. She has a body length of 10 millimetres with a shiny black globular abdomen and a distinctive red stripe down the middle.

In comparison with other countries, New Zealand has only a small number of freshwater fish. Introduced by the early settlers, salmon and trout are the best known of all fish occupying New Zealand's inland waters. Quinnat is the most common type of salmon — over five hundred thousand salmon eggs were given to New Zealand by the United States in 1901. They were first released into the Hakataramea River and Lake Ohau, and have spread widely. The main quinnat salmon rivers are now the snow-fed ones of the South Island's east coast between the Waiau in the north and the Clutha in the south. The average sized quinnat would weigh 10 kilograms and the largest recorded one taken locally weighed 29 kilograms and was caught from the Dobson River, a tributary of the Waitaki. The sock-eye and Atlantic salmon are the other two introduced species, but these have not spread as widely as the quinnat.

The rainbow and brown trout are also found in New Zealand's lakes and rivers. The rainbow has pink shading along its sides, a pale green back and spotted tail. It is mainly a lake fish and averages 50 to 60 centimetres in length and weighs 2.5 kilograms. The brown trout is one of the best known freshwater fish and is found in nearly all the main river systems of both main islands south of the Coromandel Peninsula. It forms the basis of the important river and stream fisheries.

Hunting and fishing are major attractions for both the tourist and New Zealander. Apart from trout and salmon fishing, game fishing is the special drawcard. From the Bay of Islands to the Bay of Plenty a wide selection of big fish can be found — moko, thresher and hammerhead sharks, and blue, black and striped marlin in particular.

For the intrepid huntsman, the New Zealand countryside yields game such as red deer, wapiti, sika, fallow, chamois, wild pigs and goats. Ducks, pheasant and quail are the principal game birds affording sport in New Zealand. Open seasons vary but are usually in the autumn months and extend over four weeks.

Over two thousand species of flowering plants, ferns and conifers are native to New Zealand. Most of them developed when areas of the southern hemisphere were united in one land continent, and later, when New Zealand was isolated from the other land masses, these species evolved. The New Zealand bush has undergone many changes since man first landed there. The coastal trees of both islands were originally a luxurious broadleaf type. They included pohutukawa, southern rata, ngaio, nikau palm and karaka. Clearing for settlement meant the destruction of most of these trees, but some do remain.

The inland forest has also been depleted by man's exploitation of native timber. Little remains of the luxuriant podocarp forests. The kauri dominated the bush of Coromandel and Northland — the timber was highly prized. Now only a few of these gigantic pines remain, mainly in forest parks such as Waipoua in Northland. Rimu, totara, miro, matai and kahikatea are now the dominant podocarps. Epiphytes, mosses, lichens, ferns, vines, punga and mamuka all contribute to the beauty of New Zealand forest. Beech is the other major indigenous forest, and is found in such areas as the north-west corner of the South Island, lower Westland, Fiordland and along the North Island mountain chain from East Cape to Cape Palliser.

As with the fauna, man has brought his own flora into New Zealand — exotics such as pines, poplars, gums and willows dot the countryside. Most garden plants have been introduced, but natives such as kowhai and kaka beak bring colour to the New Zealand landscape.

The unique natural variety of the land that is New Zealand makes it a wonderful country for today's New Zealanders to live in and explore and for visitors to experience.

Cape Reinga lighthouse
overlooks the meeting
place of the Tasman and
Pacific oceans. Reinga
is Maori for 'place
of leaping'. Legend has
it that the spirits
of deceased Maoris
departed from here to
their homelands in
Polynesia. (Waite)

Bathers enjoy the sweeping expanse of Matai Bay, near Cape Karikari. (Waite)
Top: *North Cape juts into the Pacific Ocean. (Kendall)*

Spirits Bay, one of the many beautiful natural beaches on the tip of the North Island. (Kendall)

Below: *Sandhills dwarf the glistening Te Paki stream. (Kendall)*

Mangonui — once a trading station and whaling base. (Waite)

Unspoilt beauty at Wainui Bay. (Kendall)

Holidaymakers at Matauri Bay. (Kendall)

Opposite: *A giant kauri reaches for the sky in Puketi Forest. (Kleinpaste)*

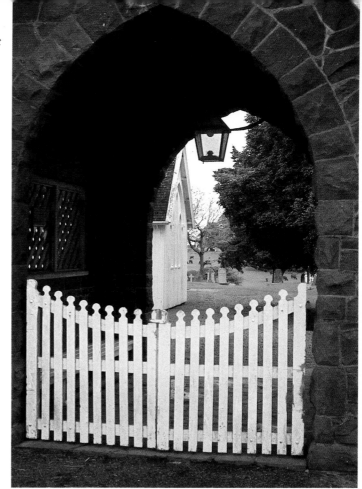

The peaceful church at Waimate North — site of the first inland European settlement. (Collinson, Kleinpaste)

Left: *Forestland on the outskirts of Waitangi. (Kleinpaste)*

Far left: *The flagstaff marks the ground on which the Treaty of Waitangi was signed. (Robinson)*

Below: *Traditional Maori carving at Waitangi. (Collinson)*

Bottom: *Waitangi Treaty House. Here, on 6 February 1840, the Maoris signed a Treaty ceding sovereignty to Queen Victoria and on 8 February the British Colony of New Zealand was proclaimed. (Robinson)*

Opposite, above: *Picturesque farmland around Kerikeri. (Kleinpaste)*

Opposite, below: *Sunset on the outskirts of Kerikeri, a flourishing citrus fruit growing centre. (Kleinpaste)*

Overleaf: *The Museum of Shipwrecks housed in an old sailing ship at Waitangi. (Kendall)*

Completed in 1836, Christ Church at Russell is the oldest surviving church in New Zealand. (Robinson)

In its heyday as a whaling centre, twenty hotels and grog shops lined the waterfront at Russell. Nowadays this picturesque town is a summer meeting place for yachts from all over New Zealand. (Prenzel)

North Head, Hokianga. (Collinson)

Opposite: *The tranquil upper reaches of the Tutukaka Harbour. (Collinson)*

Opposite: Pohutukawas frame an inlet on the Poor Knights — the northernmost group of islands in the Hauraki Gulf. (Kleinpaste)

King of the New Zealand forest — kauris at Trounson Kauri Park. (Collinson)

Below: *Game fishing off Tutukaka. (Collinson)*

Bottom: *A massive cave in the Poor Knights Islands. (Collinson)*

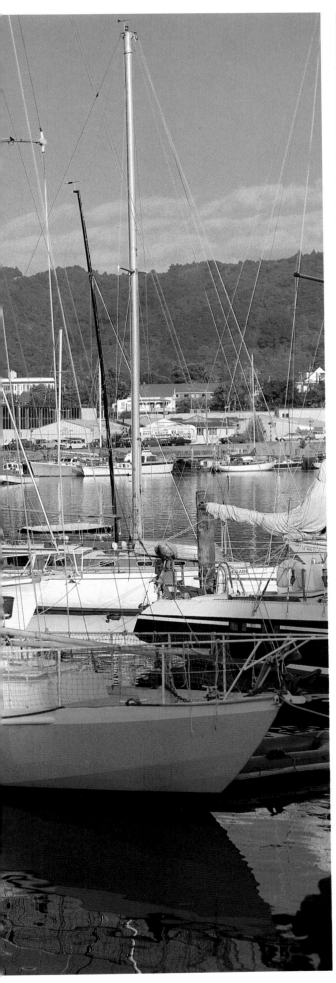

Left: *Whangarei's sheltered harbour provides moorings for both pleasure craft and commercial vessels. (Prenzel)*

The crashing Hurururu Falls at Whangarei, the only city in the Far North. (Kendall)

An old coach staging house at Kaipara Flats. (Waite)

One of the more unusual sights on the road between Auckland and Whangarei — a private house with intricate and profuse shell decorations. (Robinson)

Piha, its black iron sands washed by the Tasman, is one of the most popular West Coast beaches in Auckland. (Collinson)

Right: Aotea Square, Auckland. (Waite)

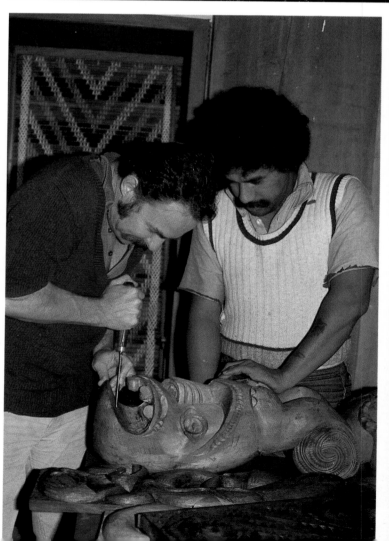

Above and top right: *The tidal waters of the Manukau Harbour form the western shores of the Auckland isthmus. (Collinson)*

The tradition of Maori carving is kept alive at Orakei, Auckland. (Waite)

The Wellesley and Queen Street intersection, Auckland. The New Zealand phenomenon — everyone crossing in different directions and at the same time. (Waite)

Auckland's grand old church — St Matthews. (Waite)

43

Motorways and overpasses weave their way in and around Auckland, New Zealand's largest city. (Kendall)

Right: *Auckland waterfront — a yachtsman's mecca. (Waite)*

Top and opposite: *The bustling Auckland waterfront is the focal point of both the commercial and leisure life of this fine city. (Prenzel)*

Showers of white clematis adorn the New Zealand bush. *(Kleinpaste)*

Cows serenely graze around an old timber shack at Kopu, scene of fierce Maori warfare on the Coromandel Peninsula. *(Kendall)*

Omahu Valley in the Coromandel Ranges. *(Kendall)*

The pohutukawa-lined road from Thames to Coromandel winds past many popular sandy beaches. (Kendall)

Below: *The Coromandel coast near Colville, once an important kauri milling district. (Kendall)*

Above: *Pohutukawas and sparkling waters at Whiritoa on the south Coromandel coast. (Kendall)*

Left: *Forest and bush line the road between Tairua and Whangamata, two popular holiday resorts. (McIvor)*

The unusually shaped Camel's Back (819 metres) in the Coromandel Ranges was the scene of a Maori battle where Ngai Terangi tribesmen were hurled to their death. (Kendall)

Rolling farmland at Coroglen on the Coromandel Peninsula. (Kendall)

51

Top left: *Extensive market gardens at Tuakau, some of the most productive farmland in the country. (Waite)*

Centre left: *There are now over sixty million sheep in New Zealand — about twenty times as many as there are people. (Collinson)*

Left: *Dairy farming is the main occupation in the lush pastoral areas surrounding the Waikato River. (Prenzel)*

Above: *Hamilton, on the banks of the Waikato River, is one of the fastest growing cities in New Zealand. (Prenzel)*

Winter at Otorohonga — set on the fertile banks of the Waipa River it is one of the best arable areas in New Zealand. (Kleinpaste)

53

Right: *The Marokopa River plummets a spectacular 36 metres over the Marokopa Falls near Waitomo. (Fairlie)*

The tuatara, found on about thirty islands off the coast of New Zealand, has an estimated life span of at least one hundred years. (Kleinpaste)

Top: *The plump native pigeon whose feathers were much prized by the Maoris for cloak decoration. (Kleinpaste)*

Centre: *Pureora Forest. (Kleinpaste)*

Bottom: *A rainbow crosses the section of Highway 1 known as the Desert Road. The area isn't a true desert but strong winds and loose gravel and sand make plant survival nearly impossible. (Kleinpaste)*

Overleaf: *A Maori child in national costume. (Kendall)*

55

2

Early Settlement

The Endeavour *approaching Otaheite*

Discovery

For centuries the Polynesians occupied the islands of New Zealand undisturbed and undiscovered. But the expanding European world, with its quest for land and riches, was not to leave them alone for long. The islands of New Zealand were once more to be fished up from the south.

The French and the Portuguese both claim the honour of discovering New Zealand but actually the Dutch are entitled to the distinction. In 1642 Captain Abel Janszoon Tasman was despatched by the Dutch East India Company 'for the discovery and exploration of the supposed southern and eastern land'. On 13 December the crews of the *Heemskirk* and *Zeeahaen* sighted a large 'high-lying land'. The vessels cast anchor in Golden Bay where, a few days later, says Tasman, 'we saw several lights on the land and four vessels coming from the shore towards us. Two of these were our own boats. The people in the other boats called to us in a loud, strong, rough voice; what they said

we did not understand; however, we called to them again in place of an answer. They repeated their cries several times; but did not come near us; they sounded also an instrument like a Moorish trumpet and we answered by blowing our own trumpet. Guns were ready prepared and small arms for an emergency, and strict watch kept.' The next day Tasman sent a boat out to make friends but a scuffle ensued and four Dutchmen were killed. Tasman pulled in the ships' anchors and sailed off, up the west coast and round the northern portion of the North Island which he called Maria Cape van Diemen after the daughter of the Governor of Batavia.

He charted part of the west coast and called the area Staten Landt, thinking it might be joined to the Staten Landt near the southern tip of South America. When the original Staten Landt was found to be an island the land was soon renamed Nieuw Zeeland, after the Dutch province. Tasman found no treasures or 'matters of great profit' and left the new country with an unfavourable impression of its inhabitants whom he found: 'bloodthirsty and prone to hostility without provocation'.

These savage inhabitants were undisturbed for yet another century until Captain James Cook rediscovered Tasman's 'Staten Landt'. Cook had been sent by the Royal Society and the Admiralty to visit Tahiti and observe the transit of Venus. After doing this he had been instructed to search for the legendary great southern land, and, failing this, to explore the coast of New Zealand.

In October 1769 Cook, in the small ship *Endeavour*, sighted the east coast of New Zealand and recorded in his Journal, 'At 2 p.m. saw land from the masthead bearing west, bearing north, which we stood directly for and could but just see it off the deck at sunset'. He called the place Poverty Bay. Cook circumnavigated the main islands and remained in New Zealand in 1769 and 1770 for one hundred and seventy-six days, surveying the coastline and observing the people. On 30 January 1770, he erected a flag post on the summit of a hill in Queen Charlotte Sound where he hoisted the Union Jack. After naming the bay where the ship was at anchor after the Queen, he took formal possession of the country in the name of His Majesty King George III.

Cook made three voyages to the South Pacific during which he visited New Zealand five different times. His first Pacific voyage added an incredible amount to world knowledge. Two distinguished botanists, Joseph Banks and Daniel Solander, were aboard the *Endeavour*. Their meticulous observations and collections added a new dimension to European botany. Cook's navigation was also superb. He proved that New Zealand, which was thought to be part 'of the imaginary southern continent, consists of two large islands divided from each other by a strait or passage of four or five leagues broad. They are situated between the latitudes of 34 degrees and 48 degrees south and between the longitude of 181 degrees and 194 degrees west from the Meridian of Greenwich'.

His charts revealed to the world a country about 1600 kilometres long and about the size of Great Britain. Its southern island had a mountainous backbone rising to over 3650 metres and its north island was extremely rugged, 'The seas, bays and rivers abound with a great variety of excellent fish, the most of them unknown in England.... In the woods are plenty of timber....' He concluded that if this country was ever settled by hardworking Europeans, 'they would soon be supplied, not only with the necessaries, but many of the luxuries of life'.

His first encounters with the Maoris were just as unfortunate as Tasman's, but with the help of an interpreter, a chieftain called Tupia who was taken aboard at Tahiti, Cook soon gained respect from this savage race.

Many explorers followed Cook. De Surville arrived two months after him in *St. Jean Baptiste* and in May 1702 Marion du Fresne anchored his two ships, *Marquis de Castries* and the *Mascarin* at the Bay of Islands to refit. Du Fresne was often ashore and struck up an amiable relationship with the Maoris. Natives and Europeans lived in harmony for a few weeks until an attack was made on the French. Twenty-eight of the party, including the commander, were killed and eaten. 'They treated us', said Lieutenant Crozet, 'with every show of friendship for thirty-three days with the intention of eating us on the twenty-fourth.' Members of the crew had desecrated sacred tribal places and the payment for this sacrilege was the lives of the strangers.

Exploitation

The knowledge of New Zealand spread; men engaged in commerce became impressed with the value of the various articles that New Zealand produced while the savant and the scientist regarded the Maori race with great interest. Also, close in the wake of the first navigators came the whalers and sealers.

In 1788 Governor Arthur Phillip founded a British Colony at Port Jackson, New South Wales. The officials, free settlers and emancipated convicts of the New South Wales settlement formed a prosperous middle class, trading on their own account. They soon began to look towards New Zealand for potential revenue. For half a century, until British sovereignty was proclaimed, New Zealand was an unofficial outpost of New South Wales. The Australian penal colony and Norfolk Island presented the only semblance of British authority in the whole south-west Pacific. New Zealand was ungoverned and became a haven for fugitives and fortune-seeking adventurers.

In 1792 the first Europeans became located in New Zealand when Captain Raven left a sealing gang at Dusky Sound. For twenty years sealers roved around the south of the South Island hunting their prey until sealing was no longer economic. In 1804 a sealer, Owen Smith, added to the geographic knowledge of the country by drawing a map showing the strait which separated Stewart Island from the South Island — Foveaux Strait. In 1810 Frederick Hasselbourgh, a British sealing captain, discovered Campbell Island.

Whaling vessels were also plying New Zealand's coastal waters for the cachelot or sperm whale. Before petroleum and paraffin became

A whaling fleet

available the oil from whale blubber and the oil stored in the head of the sperm whale were prized for fuelling lamps and candle-making. American whalers roamed at will, using the Bay of Islands as their depot.

The Bay of Islands had become the main port of the north. Whaling vessels and ships trading for timber and flax all called there for refreshments and refitting. In the full flush of the whaling trade over one hundred vessels called at the Bay of Islands in one year. The largest settlement was at Kororareka (Russell) where according to botanist John Carne Bidwill existed 'a greater number of rogues than any spot of equal size in the universe'. Ships' deserters, ex-convicts, adventurers and seamen all made up a rowdy, boisterous population. The Maori, Pomare, kept ninety-six slave girls for the enjoyment of the whaling visitors.

Each successive industry established in New Zealand, the sealing, felling and shipment of timber, whaling, the preparation of flax — each of which required the presence of European workmen on shore for considerable periods of time — led to the establishment of friendship between the Europeans and natives. This resulted in relationships which were sometimes lifelong and thus gradually prepared the country for the amicable relations that facilitated the setting up of these early small European settlements in a country that possessed so large and warlike a native population.

The Maoris were thus brought into regular contact with the Europeans over the first decade of the nineteenth century. They helped cut timber, crewed on whalers and even visited New South Wales where, as cannibals and warriors of repute they attracted intense curiosity. Trade grew, and potatoes and women were exchanged for blankets, knives and guns.

The missionaries arrive

Until 1814 there were many temporary settlements in New Zealand but nothing permanent. The first missionary settlement was established in the Bay of Islands in 1814 by Samuel Marsden, Chaplain for New South Wales.

Marsden believed that the heathen could not be converted unless they were also raised in the scale of civilisation — that they should be taught European arts and handicrafts as well as the gospel. Thus these early missionaries concentrated most of their efforts on trying to teach the Maoris practical subjects. Marsden took three missionaries with him to New Zealand: William Hall, a carpenter, John King, a shoemaker, and Thomas Kendall, a teacher.

On Christmas Day 1814 he preached the gospel in New Zealand for the first time. The natives had made rude preparations for the event by enclosing less than a quarter of a hectare of land with a fence and erecting a pulpit and reading desk, covered with native mats dyed black. Old canoes were used as seats for

59

the Europeans. Marsden writes: 'On Sunday morning when I was up on deck I saw the English flag flying, which was a pleasing sight in New Zealand. I considered it as the signal and dawn of civilisation, liberty and religion in that dark, benighted land. I never viewed the British colours with more gratification and flattered myself that they would never be removed until the natives of that land enjoyed all the happiness of British Subjects.'

Marsden's text was from the gospel of St Luke: 'Behold I bring you tidings of great joy.' After the sermon was over the natives danced their war dance. Christianity and cannibalism had come into contact.

the apparent sublimity of their [the Maoris] ideas that I have almost completely turned from a Christian to a heathen'.

The mission's first decade presented a stalemate. The missionaries found it hard to inform the Maoris of their religion and their culture. The Maoris failed to transform the missionaries into their idea of what the white man should be: traders to supply their goods.

During the 1820s changes were made. More attention was paid to the Maori language and Kendall, after producing a small Maori dictionary in 1815, took two famous chiefs, Hongi and Waikato, to England with him in 1820 to work on a transcript of the Maori language. After

The Reverend Samuel Marsden arriving at the Bay of Islands

It was difficult for the missionaries to bring their message to the Maoris. They were handicapped by their lack of knowledge of the Maori language and by the fact that they sought to teach skills that the Maori had no desire to learn. Shoe-making was of no interest to a people who did not wear shoes. Their attempts at teaching Christianity also made little progress. Their message made no sense in Maori terms of religion. The missionaries were untrained as evangelists and often unable to withstand the rigours and temptations of life in a pagan land. As Kendall wrote: 'I have been so poisoned by

Marsden dismissed Kendall and the Reverend John Butler from the mission in 1823, the Reverend Henry Williams became the new leader and introduced order and discipline into their efforts. He changed the emphasis of the mission's work away from the idea of practical example and more towards teaching. The Bible and other religious works were translated into Maori and schools for both children and adults were set up. By the 1820s the mission had three stations: the original one at Rangihoua; Kerikeri, established by Butler in 1819 and Pahia established by Williams in 1823.

Missionary teaching spread, both by book and word of mouth, and played a great part in changing the Maori way of life, in many ways hastening the decay of tribal society.

A mission station on the Waikato River

Maori meets musket

Commerce was the other major influence on Maori society. The economic frontiers of the Australian colonies were expanding rapidly in the 1820s and trading vessels probed the New Zealand market. A large trade grew in New Zealand flax which was used to make rope. In 1831 the flax trade was worth £26 000. The trade in kauri was also valuable to the Australian companies.

With the advent of commercialism the Maori way of life began to change. He abandoned his villages and moved closer to the points at which the trading vessels touched, building temporary whare alongside flax stands and near coastal stands of timber. In the South Island a new whaling industry led to the establishment of about thirty shore settlements and the Maoris settled permanently beside these stations.

The Europeans also brought disease to the Maori. Almost every explorer's landing was followed by an epidemic of a previously unknown disease. Influenza, measles, venereal disease, tuberculosis and other maladies killed tens of thousands of Maoris. But the introduction of the musket was to claim far more lives.

In the beginning, the trade goods the explorers had to offer held little attraction, but from the late eighteenth century iron and steel goods were greatly sought after. Then, from about 1815, the northern Maoris wanted guns. The Maoris had decided that the great god of the white man was the pu — the gun. By 1819 the Bay of Island Maoris had about one hundred guns and were regarded with terror by the surrounding tribes. Inter-tribal warfare increased and the Maoris of the Bay of Islands sent out a series of massive raids throughout the early 1820s. Hongi Hika, chief of Kerikeri and Waimate areas in 1821, led the largest war party ever assembled — two thousand men with about one thousand guns.

Another great and ferocious chief, Te Rauparaha of the Ngatitoa, with the aid of guns, fought his way south from Kawhia to Kapiti between 1821 and 1822. By the late 1820s many tribes had begun to build up arms and the result of this rapid acquisition of guns was a series of inter-tribal wars. At least six hundred battles are known to have occurred.

As Judge Maning recorded in a Native Land Court judgement: 'No human flesh and blood, however hardened, could endure much longer the excitement, privations, danger and unrest.... War had attained its most terrible and formidable aspect; neither age nor sex was spared; agriculture was neglected; the highest duty of man was to slay and devour his neighbour. While the combatants fought in the front, the ovens were heating in the rear. The vigorous warrior, one minute fighting hopefully in the foremost rank, exulting in his own

A Maori war canoe

61

strengths ... next moment in the glowing oven.... While his flesh is roasting the battle rages on, and at night his remains furnish a banquet for the victors and there is much boasting and great glory. Such things were.'

By the early 1840s a stalemate was reached. Most of the tribes had muskets, men were beginning to refuse to join in the fighting and missionaries persuaded many tribes to forgo their claims for revenge. Inter-tribal warfare came to a shaky halt. By then many of the Maoris had been fully drawn into the net of European commerce. In their desire for the material wealth of the Europeans they had started becoming culturally dependent on the white man — and their land was on the market.

By 1838 there were about two thousand Europeans resident in New Zealand, with about one quarter of them in the Bay of Islands. Life

First missionary house, Waimate

was rough and ready; the populace was a mixture of sober citizens, runaways and whalers, but English society had most definitely taken root. Charles Darwin wrote of the Waimate mission station in 1835:

At length we reached Waimate, after having passed over so many miles of uninhabited useless country, the sudden appearance of an English farm house and its well-dressed fields, placed there as if by an enchanter's wand, was exceedingly pleasing.... At Waimate there are three large houses where the Missionary gentlemen, Messrs: Williams, Davies and Clarke, reside; near to these are the huts of the native labourers. On an adjoining slope fine crops of barley and wheat

in full ear, and others of potatoes and of clover were standing; but I cannot attempt to describe all I saw; there were large gardens with every fruit and vegetable which England produces, and many belonging to a warmer clime. I may instance asparagus, kidney beans, cucumbers, rhubarb, apples and pears, figs, peaches, apricots, grapes, olives, gooseberries, currants, hops, gorse for fences and English oaks! and many different kinds of flowers.... Around the farmyard were stables, a threshing barn with its winnowing machine, a blacksmith's forge, and on the ground ploughshares and other tools; in the middle was that happy mixture of pigs and poultry which may be seen so comfortably lying together in every English farm yard. At the distance of a few hundred yards, where the water of a little rill has been dammed up into a pool, a large and substantial water mill had been erected. All this is very surprising when it is considered that five years ago, nothing but the fern here flourished. Moreover, native workmanship, taught by the Missionaries, has effected this change:- the lesson of the Missionarie is the enchanter's wand. The house has been built, the windows framed, the fields ploughed, and even the trees grafted by the New Zealander. At the mill a New Zealander may be seen powdered white with flour like his brother miller in England.

Annexation by Britain

Sealers, whalers and flax and timber traders had all flocked into the country after Cook made New Zealand's resources known to the world. The new land and its people had been exploited. The Maoris had been introduced to disease, liquor, prostitution — and the musket — and the population was greatly decreased and the social system changed. The gentler influence of the missionaries had been offset by the more commercial and rougher influences of the traders.

It was time to take stock — to find ways to protect the Europeans from the savagery of the Maoris and to protect the Maoris from white depravity that often accompanied early settlement. News of atrocities — both European and Maori — had reached New South Wales and Britain. Perhaps the most outrageous event occurred when Captain John Stewart on the brig *Elizabeth* ferried chief Te Rauparaha and a war party from Kapiti Island to Akaroa, where, with his help, they massacred a population of a pa. All in return for a cargo of flax.

Law and order was difficult to establish and maintain. Early Australian governors had vague powers of representation in the adjacent islands and in 1823 the jurisdiction of Australia's courts had been extended to New Zealand. Legal difficulties such as obtaining long-distance witnesses and delays in investigating offences rendered this jurisdiction practically unenforceable.

Britain had to step in — she had good reason to. Humanitarians back home were agitating for the protection of the Maoris from the European's 'contaminating influences'. She was afraid that her traditional rival, France, would acquire a toehold close to her Pacific colonies and the newly formed New Zealand Company was pressurising her to colonise the country.

The British Government with its already vast empire was reluctant to commit itself to further responsibilities. But the pressure was upon them. Hesitantly, in 1833, they sent James Busby over from New South Wales and he was appointed British Resident at Waitangi. His tasks were to protect the Maori from the British adventurer, to send escaped convicts back for trial, to encourage trade and to assist settlers. He had a moral duty to do these things but was given neither the magisterial power nor the armed forces which might have enabled him to carry out these tasks. The terms of his appointment were unfavourable in many respects: he had no security of employment, and no official residence — only a prefabricated frame shipped to New Zealand.

The whole exercise was futile — no one in New Zealand except Busby took the residency seriously and it was inconceivable that he should succeed. His only real achievement was in 1835 when he persuaded thirty-five chiefs to proclaim themselves the 'United Tribes of New Zealand'. They declared they were the heads of a sovereign state and announced that they would have annual meetings to determine the welfare of their realm. Busby called this 'New Zealand's magna carta'.

His reason for this declaration of independence was not really well-thought out. In 1835 Busby learnt that Charles de Thierry, self-styled 'Baron' and 'sovereign chief of New Zealand, King of Nukuheva' was about to land in New Zealand with a considerable following and the intention of possessing lands. Within thirty-six hours of receiving this news, Busby outlined his plan to set up the United Tribes of New Zealand.

In a letter to de Thierry Busby stated that the United Tribes of New Zealand had reaffirmed their independence and that if de Thierry attempted to assert his claims within New Zealand he would meet 'the most spirited resistance from a population well supplied with arms and ammunition'. Although it was ridiculed in New South Wales as 'a paper pellet fired off at Baron de Thierry', the attribution of sovereignty to the Maori chiefs remained the basis of British policy in New Zealand until 1840.

de Thierry's plans were hopelessly grandiose and although he did acquire some land he never managed to reign New Zealand. At a later date, after the signing of the Treaty of Waitangi, Governor Hobson was to tersely write to him: 'the only Sovereign Chief who can be acknowledged as such from the date of the Treaty is Her Majesty Queen Victoria.... To suppose such an anomaly as every man being the Sovereign of his acre or ten thousand acres, is really so absurd that it admits of no argument between civilised and educated men'.

Busby House

Busby had ambitious plans for New Zealand: education for the Maoris, the founding of a Maori newspaper and the setting aside of reservation land at a time when the Maoris were selling excessive amounts of land in return for trade articles. He even proposed a council of settlers, missionaries and Maoris to advise the Resident. But his authority was non-existent. Generally, when settlers asked him to bring justice against criminals he had to reply that he was powerless, not even being vested with the powers of a magistrate. The situation grew more and more out of control. Speculators were flooding the country and huge areas of land were allegedly being purchased for a few muskets and blankets. One Australian syndicate purchased the entire South Island, with Stewart Island thrown in, all for a few hundred pounds.

In 1837 two hundred settlers petitioned the British Government to afford them protection. Citizens formed temperance societies and vigilance committees to try and control the situation themselves. One group, the Kororareka Association, arose to administer 'lynch law', its members having adapted themselves to a society where, as Busby wrote, 'the only law was that of the strong arm'. New Zealand clamoured for British intervention and however determined Britain was to pursue a policy of minimum intervention, complete annexation could not be avoided.

Action finally came on 29 January 1840 when the Colonial Office dispensed with Busby's services and appointed Captain William Hobson as Lieutenant-Governor. Hobson's duties were to negotiate with the Chiefs for the transfer of sovereignty to the British Crown with the 'free and intelligent consent of the natives', to induce the chiefs to contract that no lands should in future be sold except to the Crown; to announce by proclamation that no title to land acquired from the natives of the dependency would be recognised unless confirmed by a Crown grant; to arrange for the appointment of a commission to determine what lands held by British subjects had been lawfully acquired and to appoint a Protector to supervise the interests of the Maori population.

It was a formidable task. Hobson had to bridge the wide gap between the two cultures and somehow get the Maoris to understand the concept of 'sovereignty'. With the help of Henry Williams who knew the native language well, a document had to be drawn up that would both establish British sovereignty and attempt to protect the Maori people from any adverse effects of colonisation. The Treaty of Waitangi — perhaps the most important single document in the history of New Zealand and over the years to become the subject of bitter controversy — was thus drawn up and translated into Maori by Henry Williams. It can be condensed as follows:

... the Queen of England, in her regard for the Maori people, desiring to preserve for them their rights as chiefs and the possession of their lands, and also — having heard that many of her subjects had settled in New Zealand, and that more were about to follow — to prevent troubles arising between the two races, had thought it right to send William Hobson, a captain in the Royal Navy, to be a Governor for all parts of New Zealand now or hereafter ceded to her; to carry into effect which object the following articles of agreement are proposed:-

I.   The chiefs of New Zealand cede to the Queen forever the right of government over the whole of New Zealand.

II.   Her Majesty the Queen of England confirms and guarantees to the chiefs and tribes of New Zealand, and to the respective families and individuals thereof, the full, exclusive and undisturbed possession of their lands and estates, forests and fisheries, and other properties which they may collectively and individually possess, so long as it is their wish and desire to retain the same in their possession. But the chiefs of the united tribes and the individual chiefs, yield to Her Majesty the exclusive right of pre-emption over such lands as the proprietors may be disposed to alienate, at such prices as may be agreed upon between the respective proprietors and persons appointed by Her Majesty to treat with them on her behalf.

III.   In consideration for consent to the Queen's Government, the Queen will protect all the Maori people and give them all the rights and privileges of British subjects.

The Treaty Monument

Under this Treaty, however, the natives not merely ceded to the Queen the right to purchase such land as the owners were willing to sell, but 'the pre-emptive right of selection over all lands', and the practical interpretation put upon this by each of the early Governors except Fitzroy was that the Queen might have the refusal of all lands that the natives were willing to sell and if that refusal were given no one else would be allowed to buy. This was one of the chief grievances that underlay the Maori disaffection of the future.

The Treaty was presented to a large gathering of Maoris on 5 February 1840. Long, animated discussion followed, not all of it running smoothly. Several powerful chiefs urged their people not to sign the agreement. Said one: 'Do not sign the paper, if you do, you will be reduced to the condition of slaves, your land will be taken from you and your dignity as chiefs will be destroyed.' Other equally powerful chiefs countered these remarks. 'The native mind cannot understand these things,' said Hone Heke, 'they must trust the advice of their missionaries.' On the following morning, 6 February 1840, a consensus was reached and the Treaty signed by Governor Hobson and forty-six head chiefs, closely followed by many others. 'We are now one people,' said Hobson.

Hobson made copies of the Treaty and had them carried throughout the countryside for the collection of signatures and eventually most of the leading chieftains signed. The Treaty was accepted in good faith by all concerned and carried obligations on both sides to build a biracial community in New Zealand.

On 21 May Hobson proclaimed British sovereignty over the whole country; the North Island on the grounds of cession by the Maoris and the South Island by right of discovery. New Zealand was at last British.

The early settlements

Edward Gibbon Wakefield's theories on 'systematic colonisation' were the motivating force behind the New Zealand Association — later to become the New Zealand Company. Wakefield believed that land should be sold at a fixed price, high enough to prevent labourers becoming land owners until they had worked and saved for several years, and that this would foster concentrated, civilised settlements. Revenue from the land sales would be used to select assisted emigrants from the labouring classes so there would be an assured supply of labour, thus attracting the capitalist-farmer. Wakefield believed that this would strike a balance between land, labour and capital and the new colony would flourish.

In 1836 Wakefield described New Zealand to the House of Commons as 'the fittest country in the world for colonisation', and regretted that it was being settled 'in a most slovenly, scrambling and disgraceful manner'. In 1837 the New Zealand Association was formed to colonise New Zealand along the lines that Wakefield proposed. They attempted to carry a private member's Bill through Parliament to achieve their objectives, but a combination of lack of Government support and the humanitarians' belief that this type of settlement would afford no protection to the natives of New Zealand led to its defeat.

The Association was dissolved and the New Zealand Company formed. This Company agreed to Government stipulations that they provide their own capital and obtain Maori consent for settlement but when attempting to apply for a Charter they were told that they could not be recognised until New Zealand was annexed. When these colonisers heard that the

Government intended to forbid all private purchase of land once sovereignty had been proclaimed they decided to act on their own initiative and promptly defied British policy by despatching Colonel William Wakefield on the *Tory* to buy land for settlement at Wellington and elsewhere.

The battle between imperialism and humanitarianism began. Even before the *Tory* arrived in New Zealand the scramble by the New Zealand Company to recruit settlers had begun.

prepared. Harsh reality awaited these settlers when they arrived in Wellington.

The settlement of Wellington

Five ships carrying over eight hundred people left England before it was even known if the New Zealand Company had purchased a site in Wellington. It was a bold act of faith. As one early resident, H. W. Petre, wrote in 1841:

Wellington

Land was 'sold' and passenger ships despatched. The public were informed that New Zealand was a paradise, economic prospects were unlimited and all types of commerce were possible. The Company's advertising was designed to attract 'men of refinement', men who once experiencing the deprivations that in reality did exist soon moved on. Absentee land owning and land speculation was commonplace. Landorders were being sold at £1 an acre in landorder lots of one hundred and one acres and the Company sold one thousand of these in 1839 before the Wellington site had even been

'Before any intelligence was received from Colonel Wakefield, emigrant ships sailed from England with orders to touch at Port Hardy in D'Urvilles Island for directions, which it was expected that Colonel Wakefield would convey thither, for proceeding to their ultimate destination. This was a bold proceeding on the part of the Company and still more so on that of the emigrants.'

Disorganisation greeted these first settlers: the land suited for settlement was limited, the Company's title to the land was questionable and the Maoris were, at first, the cause of some

66

alarm. There were, however, some compensations. 'Food was abundant and very cheap,' wrote Helen Simpson in *The Women of New Zealand*. 'Letters from the earliest arrivals remark "the Quantities of fish of various kinds, of the pigeons twice as large as our English ones", the pork, the potatoes, Indian corn and native greens — "A piece of pigtail tobacco weighing one ounce, value threepence, brings a basket of potatoes weighing about thirty pounds, including the basket made of flax. One native offered us a very large pig, nearly ten stone, for a shark-hook worth a shilling, but we disclaimed to take advantage of them, but they afterwards sold their pig for two shirts ..."'

And with the help of Maori natives, building began. According to H. W. Petre: 'Our first habitation consisted entirely of very rude huts built by ourselves. At a later period after the arrival of other emigrant ships, the Natives rendered valuable assistance in this sort of work, at which they are very expert.... Many of them deserved to be called houses, and were, when I quitted Port Nicholson still used by emigrants of all classes.'

Nelson

By 1841 two hundred houses had been built, but there were over two thousand inhabitants. This housing shortage, along with commerce and trade, provided many sources of employment. By July 1840, the town acres had been laid out and selected and much later, in June 1841, the hundred-acre country sections were surveyed. Wellington flourished. In 1850 when Charlotte Godley landed there she wrote, 'the town surpasssed my expectations in every way. It is really uncommonly pretty, and with very good comfortable houses, although certainly no fine buildings, but they are generally built with a gable on to the street, which looks very picturesque, and there is an almost continuous row along the beach for about two miles, something like the bit of Hastings which joins the old on to the new town, with a patch at each end of level ground; one is getting very full of houses with barracks, a new church, a meeting house etc., and the other which is at the west end, where we live, is used for cricket, flying kites, soldiers exercising etc....'

The settlement of Nelson

Nelson was the second of the ambitious New Zealand Company's settlements. Captain Arthur Wakefield headed the settlement, and the first ship, the *Fifeshire*, arrived in Nelson on 1 February 1842. The normal problems ensued. Much of the land was useless and many of the settlers were ignorant of farming. By 1842 it was estimated that an extra fifty thousand acres (about 20 200 hectares) of land would be required to complete the original settlement scheme, but where was this land to be found? Later that year an easy pass was discovered into the Wairau Valley and surveyors were sent in. The Maoris considered this move tantamount to occupation and the chiefs Te Rauparaha and Te Rangihaeata arrived to object.

This culminated in a confrontation between a party led by Captain Wakefield and the Maoris. Tempers flared, a gun accidentally fired and strife broke out, ending in the death of a number of pakehas and the capture and later massacre of a large number of Nelson's most capable settlers, including Captain Wakefield. Governor Fitzroy arrived to mediate in the dispute and passed the verdict that the natives had never sold the land to the Europeans. He said:

> Hearken, O chiefs and elder men, to my decision. In the first place the pakehas were in the wrong; they had no right to build houses upon the land, the sale of which you disputed ... they were wrong in trying to apprehend you, who had committed no crime.... As they were greatly to blame, and as they brought on and began the fight, and as you were hurried into crime by their misconduct, I will not avenge their deaths.

The Wairau massacre marked a low point in the life of the Nelson settlers but after weathering some financial and political storms the settlement eventually consolidated.

Christchurch in 1852

The settlement of Christchurch and Dunedin

Wakefield's New Zealand Company's work of colonising on 'systematic' principles was continued by two new associations which founded Otago in 1848 and Canterbury in 1850.

On 23 March 1848 the *John Wickliffe*, chartered by the Lay Association of the Free Church of Scotland to bring settlers to Otago, dropped anchor at Port Chalmers. The settlement was the result of three things: Wakefield's colonising ideas, the emergence of the Free Church of Scotland and the economic and social conditions in Scotland in the 1840s. The original promoter of the Otago scheme, George Rennie, had been supplanted by Captain William Cargill and the Reverend Thomas Burns who set out to establish a Free Church settlement where 'piety, rectitude and industry' would have a place. Settlement began and by December 1848 much progress had been made. The *Otago News* reported:

... now, instead of seeing one or two solitary houses, with a narrow swamp footpath, the eye is gladdened with a goodly sprinkling of houses, some of wood, others of mud and grass; whilst numerous gardens, well fenced and cleared, and one street at least showing a broad track from end to end of the future town gives evidence of the progress we have made. We have two hotels, a church, a school, a wharf small though it be. We have butchers, bakers and stores of all descriptions. We have an Odd Fellows' Society — a Cricket Club — we have boats plying on the bay and the river and every outward sign of commercial activity and enterprise.

Dunedin

Settlers continued to arrive and by the end of the first year Dunedin had a population of seven hundred and forty-five. These first settlers succeeded in stamping upon Otago a character which lasted for generations. This was the prominent place of the Presbyterian Church, the emphasis on education and the general Scottish cultural flavour.

Christchurch was also a church settlement. In 1848 the idea of a church settlement was formally approved in London and the newly formed Canterbury Association, with the help of the New Zealand Company bought land from the Maoris in Canterbury. Their leader was John Robert Godley and the 'pilgrim' settlers embarked upon finding their promised land. The first four ships, *Charlotte Jane, Sir George Seymour, Randolph* and *Cressy*, brought a large number of sound, well-educated men that were to strengthen the advantages already inherent in the new settlement: a spacious alluvial plain and very few Maoris.

Three town sites were chosen and surveyed — Lyttleton, Christchurch and Sumner — and preliminary work had been done on building and development before the arrival of the Canterbury Association 'pilgrims'. 'The land we passed,' wrote Edward Ward as the *Charlotte Jane* was nearing Lyttleton, 'was most beautifully situated — high and wooded, with glades of grass running up through the forest here and there. We were all enchanted as fresh beauties

stone of Christs College was laid in 1857. Social life flourished: Mrs Godley reported in March 1851 that a friend of hers was about to give a ball: 'a bread and butter ball, that is to say, without any attempt at a grand supper, champagne or indeed wine at all.... We have been very anxious that some such beginning should be made because it is really, here, very desirable that there should be occasional meetings; it does people so much good to rub against others....'.

High Street, Christchurch

broke upon our view every moment.... As we rounded to, we shot past a little point of land, and the town of Lyttleton burst upon our view — like a little village — but nothing more than a village — in snugness, neatness, and pretty situation.'

It was good country for sheep and cattle. As early as 1844 the Deans brothers were milking cows and selling bullocks and butter to the Wellington settlement. Most of the richer settlers who came out on the Canterbury Association ships became run holders when the rural sections were surveyed. By 1858 all the land purchased by the Canterbury Association had been taken up.

Meanwhile, Christchurch was emerging as a fashionable town. The first Anglican Church was opened on 20 July 1851 and the corner-

The settlement of Auckland

The 'Wakefield Settlement' plan was the backbone of the above settlements — of New Zealand's four main centres, Christchurch, Dunedin, Wellington and Auckland, it was only the latter that did not come under the influence of the scheme.

In 1840 the land where Auckland now lies was very sparsely populated; Maori inhabitants were few and there were scarcely any European settlers. It was not until after the signing of the Treaty of Waitangi that attention was paid to this part of New Zealand. Hobson needed a new site for his capital — Kororareka in the Bay of Islands was flawed by notoriety and too remote. The Wellington settlement was considered unacceptable as it would appear to sanc-

Auckland Harbour

tion the New Zealand Company and its irregular land purchases. The missionary Henry Williams suggested the Taranaki Isthmus to Hobson and he set out to inspect it. After careful examination he made his choice: 'the south side of the Waitemata in the district of Thames'.

On 15 September 1840 the barque *Anna Watson* arrived to set up the capital. On 18 September the flag was run up and the settlement founded. Writes a Mrs Mathew: 'Her Majesty's health was most rapturously drunk with cheers long and loud ... to the evident delight of the natives.' Settlers began to flow in to the new capital from other parts of New Zealand and from Australia, and the first Government auction of land was held on 19 April 1841.

From the very beginning this new settlement differed from the other New Zealand settlements. The community was unplanned, comprising mainly a random inflow of settlers with very few organised groups of immigrants and the settlement heavily depended on the financial well-being of the Government. The Maoris were the greatest economic asset of the struggling community. They provided cheap staple labour for the building of houses and clearing of land. The money they earned went back into the community — they spent freely on blankets, clothing and iron tools. By 1851 Auckland was emerging from its pioneer phase — the area had 33 per cent of New Zealand's population and provided 43 per cent of the public revenue.

New Zealand was settled in a number of ways. Apart from the organised settlements of the 'Wakefield Scheme' there were military settlements, communities established by groups of compatriots such as the Bohemians at Waipu and the French at Akaroa; land speculators, squatters, traders and missionaries all had their part to play. Settlements, too, grew up at ran-

70

dom on harbours — Napier and Gisborne — on navigable rivers, for example, Dargaville, and some towns became established where there was already a Maori village.

The New Zealand Company did, however, play the most notorious role in the settlement of New Zealand. By the mid-1840s the four main Company settlements all had their problems. Labour and capital were unbalanced and many settlers left. Others turned against the Company, damning it for its misleading propaganda. A legacy of racial bitterness was created by the misunderstandings over land procurement. Land was the biggest problem. Hobson instituted a scrutiny of pre-Waitangi land claims that kept the settlers in a constant state of uncertainty. William Spain, a London lawyer, was sent to decide the validity of the Company's land purchases and found that only a small proportion of the 20 000 000 acres (about 8 100 000 hectares) claimed by Colonel Wakefield had been fairly purchased. The first few years of Company settlement saw fighting or the threat of war between Maori and the Company over disputed land claims which boded ill for the future.

After 1844 the Company was in decline with mounting debts. It was given a large Government loan on the security of its lands in 1845, but even this was not enough. In 1850 the Company ceased to act as a colonising body and surrendered its charter. The Crown came into possession of the Company's land and paid to the shareholders their original capital and a small dividend. Colonisation had proved to be a poor business proposition — the theory was laudable but they had largely failed in the practice. To the Company's credit, from May 1839 to January 1843 it had despatched fifty-seven ships carrying nineteen thousand migrants to New Zealand but in the final analysis it was random migration that provided the bulk of New Zealand's European population. On the collapse of the Company, provincial governments assumed the mantle of coloniser.

A state is founded

Settlement had drastically increased but in 1845 the British Government had still made little impression and the financially depressed administration and disputed land titles left New Zealand in a raw, disordered condition. In this year, George Grey was appointed Governor of New Zealand and the quality of administration began to improve.

A liberal, Grey wanted to provide New Zealand with a system of democratic government. From the start of British rule in New Zealand in 1840 the country was administered through a resident governor by the Colonial Secretary in London. The settlers, led by the New Zealand Company, began to agitate for self-government and in 1846 Earl Grey despatched an elaborate constitution. The Governor, however, wanting self-government, but trying to postpone the enactment of the constitution as he felt that it was dangerous to give the European minority power to rule the Maori majority, delayed the move, intending to create a Provincial system of government for the period of suspension of the constitution until he felt the time was right for self-government.

New Zealand was separated into two provinces: New Ulster in the north and New Munster in the south. This did not suit the settlers who still preached the doctrines of responsible government. By 1852 Grey's new drafts for a constitution, the settlers' proposals and British views all combined to create an extremely democratic formal constitution: the six Provincial Councils (Wellington, Nelson, Auckland, Canterbury, Otago and New Plymouth), the House of Representatives, and the Superintendents of the Provinces were all elective and the members of the Legislative Council (the Upper House) were nominated for life by the Governor.

The new constitution gave wide voting rights, although as the franchise was based on property, almost all the Maoris and a few Europeans were excluded. The Governor remained in control at the centre, subject only to instructions from the British Government. The new constitution was brought into effect with turbulent elections and by the end of 1853 the provincial governments were established. Grey departed for the governorship at Cape Town in 1853 — without calling together the central Parliament. Colonel Robert Wynyard took over as acting Governor and in May 1854 first assembled Parliament.

The Parliament did not achieve order and system until 1856 when the financial relations of the Provincial and central governments were settled and the government of New Zealand became threefold: local services were handled by the regional authorities; oversight of the Provinces and various central functions were the role of the colonial government; and matters of imperial concern such as external defence remained with the British Government. The Provinces, for the next two decades, probably affected the lives of the settlers more than the acts of the General Assembly. They were to a certain degree self-governing and each kept the proceeds of the land sales. They appointed agents in England to entice migrants, drew up regulations for land use and employed road gangs to open up the land.

To some extent the Assembly was divided over the degree of power to be given to the Provincial and central governments respectively. By 1876, the central government had become more consolidated and the Provinces had lost control of public works, railways and immigration. The central government had taken over their debts and refused to allow them to raise loans. The Provinces could hardly justify their existence and Vogel abolished the system of Provincial government.

The Provincial system proved to be an interim measure until a united colony could be formed. It was, however, not until 1947 that New Zealand acquired her final legal powers — the power to amend her own constitution and to pass laws inconsistent with British legislation that applied to New Zealand.

The Legislative Council was voted out of existence and since then the one elected 'lower' house has governed as Parliament.

Government House

The poi dance, performed by a Maori Concert Party at Rotorua. (Kendall)

Pastoral scene at Mamaku in the central North Island. (Kendall)

73

A Maori meeting house at Ohinemutu. These carved meeting houses were the most elaborate buildings found in any Polynesian society. (Kendall)

Top: *Lake Rotorua, the largest of the many lakes in this region, is the setting of the famous love story of Hinemoa and Tutanekai, who lived on the enchanting Mokoia Island in the centre of the lake. (Collinson)*

The Tudor-style St Faiths Anglican Church at Ohinemutu was built in 1910. (Kendall)

Two unusual and subtly coloured thermal spectacles,
*(**opposite**) Bridal Veil Falls at Waiatapu, and (**right**)*
the Golden Fleece Terrace at Orakei Korako.
(Waite, Collinson)

Green terraces at Orakei Korako. (Collinson)

Right: *The steaming Cathedral Cliffs surround a crater holding a hot bubbling lake. (Kendall)*

Silica terraces at Orakei Korako. (Collinson)

Fishing the outlet at Lake Tarawera. (Collinson)

Opposite: *New Zealand's longest river, the Waikato (425 kilometres), near Broadlands. The river runs from its source on Mt Ruapehu to the Tasman Sea, south of Auckland. (Collinson)*

Opposite, above: *Aratiatia Rapids, where the Waikato drops 28 metres in 800 metres. (Collinson)*

Opposite, below: *The harnessing of geothermal power in the volcanic area. (Collinson)*

Above: *Sunset over Lake Taupo, New Zealand's largest lake covering 616 square kilometres. Once an active volcano, the shores today are peaceful. (Collinson)*

Left: *After leaving Lake Taupo the Waikato River hurtles over the Huka Falls. (Robinson)*

Sunset over the lower slopes of Mt Ruapehu. (Collinson)

Left and opposite, above:
Mt Ruapehu, at 2796 metres, is the highest mountain in the North Island and an extremely popular ski resort. (Collinson, White)

The almost perfect cone of Mt Ngauruhoe viewed from Mt Ruapehu. (Kleinpaste)

Overleaf: *The perpetually snow-capped Mt Ruapehu is an active volcano with a simmering crater lake. (Prenzel)*

The Tongariro River, one of New Zealand's favourite trout fishing spots, enters Lake Taupo through five streams. (Collinson)

Opposite, above left: *A man-made waterfall in the beautiful Pukekura Park, New Plymouth. (Kendall)*

Opposite, above right: *Spring comes to the central North Island, north of Taihape. (Kendall)*

Opposite, below: *Pukekura Park, New Plymouth — its Victorian charm makes it one of the finest parks in the country. (Newman)*

Mt Ngauruhoe viewed from the Desert Road. (Prenzel)

Above and right: *The now dormant Mt Egmont, formed about seventy thousand years ago, is the largest in the chain of volcanoes in Taranaki. (Prenzel)*

Opposite, above: *Maori rock drawings adorn the eroded caves at the small fishing settlement of Tongaporutu near New Plymouth. (Fairlie)*

Opposite, below: *The Wanganui River dissects the city of Wanganui, which was founded in 1840 and is now the regional centre for small industries and commerce. (Newman)*

Left: *The Durie Hill War Memorial, Wanganui. (Newman)*

The solitude of the fisherman at Matata in the Bay of Plenty. (Kendall)

The turbulent waters of the Rangitaiki River have been harnessed for hydro-electricity. The waters back up for 19 kilometres behind the large earth dam at Matahina. (Waite)

Right: *Sunset over the upper Ohiwa Harbour in the Bay of Plenty. (Kendall)*

90

Above: *White Island, 50 kilometres offshore from Whakatane, is an active volcano often hidden by clouds of steam. Over thirty eruptions have been recorded since 1826. (Kendall)*

Ohope Beach, near Whakatane, one of the most popular seaside resorts in the North Island. (Kendall)

Overleaf: *The Raukokore River flows out to a coast that was once plied by whaling boats. (Kendall)*

91

The Motu River mouth — Motu means 'isolated place' in Maori. Further inland the stream is popular for trout fishing. (Kendall)

Captain Cook named this area the Bay of Plenty — a name justified by the warm climate, beautiful beaches and verdant vegetation of this crescent-shaped area. (Kendall)

Waves crash over rocks at Hicks Bay, named by Cook after his Lieutenant, Zachary Hicks. (Kendall)

Opposite above: *The cliffs of Tolaga Bay. 'The country is agreeable beyond description, and, with proper cultivation, might be rendered a second kind of Paradise,' wrote Sydney Parkinson, an artist on Cook's voyage to this area. (Kendall)*

Opposite, below: *Te Araroa, scene of a bloody tribal battle were nearly three thousand Maoris met their death. (Kendall)*

A rainbow lights up
the sky at Tuai near
Lake Waikaremoana.
(Kendall)

An old jetty stretches
into the water at Tolaga
Bay. Cook's botanists,
Banks and Solander,
made one of their first
collections of New
Zealand flora and fauna
in this area. (Kendall)

*Cape Kidnappers —
the only known mainland
nesting site of the
Australasian gannet.
Over 4500 birds nest at
the 3 sanctuaries within
this area. (Waite)*

*Napier, first settled
as a trading station in
the late 1830s, was
nearly demolished by
earthquake and fire in
1931. The town has
been rebuilt to resist
earthquakes. (Waite)*

Centrepoint at Masterton, the largest town in the Wairarapa. (Waite)

Turakirae Head, east of Wellington, is made up of five terraces — old beaches that have successively been raised above sea level. (Kleinpaste)

The Orongorongo Ranges, a trampers' paradise near Wellington. (Kleinpaste)

Bottom: *Cape Terawhiti overlooking Cook Strait to the west of Wellington. (Kleinpaste)*

A giant weta — these insects have a fossil history dating back one hundred and ninety million years. (Kleinpaste)

One of Wellington's most famous trademarks, the quaint cable-car winches passengers 122 metres above the city to the mellow suburb of Kelburn. (Prenzel)

Wellington — the nation's capital, named after the Duke of Wellington. In 1842 it was the first New Zealand town to become a Borough. (Waite)

This page and overleaf: *One of the most picturesque cities in New Zealand with hills tumbling down to a glistening harbour, the site of Wellington, according to Maori legend, was first discovered by Polynesian navigators Kupe and Ngahue. (Prenzel, Waite)*

The Cook Strait ferry regularly plies its way between Wellington and Picton, connecting the two islands. (Robinson)

3

The Nation Emerges

Government buildings, Wellington

The Maori, the land and the wars

To the Maori, the land of New Zealand was Papa — the Earth Mother. His spiritual well being was deeply linked with it and his material culture founded on it. Land changed hands only by conquest and was owned by tribes, not by the indivdual.

In the beginning the Maoris did not really understand the full meaning of the sale of their land. During the signing of the Treaty of Waitangi one chief remarked that they were merely transferring the 'shadow of the land' to Queen Victoria and the 'substance of the land remains with us'. The Treaty gave the Crown the sole right to buy land from the Maoris and as more and more settlers poured into New Zealand the Maoris became increasingly reluctant to sell. A clash between Maori and settler was inevitable: the aspirations of the Maori and settler were incompatible.

Fighting first broke out in 1843 when settlers attempted to survey land in the Wairau Valley long before their disputed title was investigated by the Lands Commissioner. The next major outbreaks of fighting were in Northland in 1844 — strangely enough, not as a direct result of land disputes. Hone Heke, the first Maori to

sign the Treaty of Waitangi, had changed allegiances and showed what he thought of British sovereignty by cutting down its symbol — the flagstaff at Kororareka — and then sacking the town. Heke had countless grievances. The foundation of Auckland as capital had left Kororareka almost a ghost town; customs duties discouraged trading vessels from calling and there was a rapid decline of Maori earnings from trade.

Overriding this was the belief that the Treaty of Waitangi had been treacherous: the mana of the land had been passed to the Queen and the Maori people had become slaves. Or, as another chief put it; 'the substance of the land goes to the Europeans, the shadow only will be our portion'. Heke thought in terms of a Maori identity. He pleaded that two flags, the Maori and the British, should fly side by side. About a thousand Maoris under Heke and Kawiti took arms against the British and the dissatisfaction of the northern Maoris flared into warfare. Governor Fitzroy persuaded about twenty chiefs to lay down their arms, but after Heke again cut down the flagstaff on 10 January 1845 the situation became critical and for over a year skirmishes ravaged the far north.

Fitzroy vacillated in his treatment of these

Hone Heke

ing the settlers with instant death if they made any noise or attempted to give the alarm.

On 3 March 1846 the raiders attacked British troops at Taita and Grey declared martial law. A strong force of British soldiers occupied the Hutt Valley and in August, after a series of hard-fought battles, the Maoris were forced to retreat. The Hutt Valley Maoris had fought desperately to preserve their rights, but the odds proved overwhelming.

For a time after this, apart from an attack led by Te Mamaku on the town of Wanganui, the fighting was over. Grey did much to keep the shaky peace between Maori and pakeha. He instituted a method of negotiating land purchases that was in accordance with Maori custom: Land Purchase Commissioners would discuss ownership and price at tribal meetings and large numbers of Maoris would sign the deed of sale. Large areas of land were bought in the North Island and almost the whole of the South Island was acquired. Taranaki in the North Island proved to be the only stumbling block.

In 1848, five hundred Maoris who had previously been living in exile on the outskirts of Wellington returned to their homelands in Taranaki. Their chief, Wiremu Kingi (William King), refused to settle where Grey wanted him

uprisings and it was not until Governor Grey replaced him that the war was ended. Grey drove Kawiti out of his pa and made peace. Heke was left alone, but he had lost his will to fight, and fought no more.

Two more disturbances, at Wellington and Wanganui, were quelled by Grey. The Maori tribes in the Hutt area, under the leadership of Te Rangihaeata, were plundering and destroying settlers' homes. Land was most definitely the reason this time. Genial initial relations between settler and Maori had deteriorated. Disputes and superstitions surrounded many land transactions and the validity of the Maori vendor's title to the land was not always closely examined. Te Rangihaeata, a firm upholder of the belief that the land was essential to the mana of chiefs, began a series of raids, stripping the settlers of their possessions. The *Independent*, Wellington's newspaper, reported:

What they were not able to carry away, they wantonly destroyed on the spot, breaking the furniture, demolishing the windows and committing all sort of outrages and threaten-

Wanganui

106

to and declined to sell any of his land. He said, 'I will not give up my land until I am first dragged by my hair and put in gaol.' Immigration decreased in this area and the cry 'Taranaki wants more land' went up from the settlers. In 1855 the *Taranaki Herald* remarked, 'The feeling generated in the mind of the actual settler who is compelled to go miles back into the forest because he cannot obtain land, is one extremely unfavourable to continued peaceable relations with the Natives; and with the growth of European populations and the increased pressure for land, this feeling will become more bitter.'

Grey failed to solve this Taranaki land problem, but by the early 1850s he was convinced that a basis for peaceful co-existence had been established. The Maoris superficially appeared to be adapting to their new life: they owned most of the coastal shipping, and they grew, sold and exported potatoes, wheat and other foodstuffs. They were given Government loans and by 1852 some seven hundred Maoris were attending Government subsidised schools. Hospitals gave free treatment. Maoris found ready urban employment on public works and other tasks. However, the majority of Maoris still lived in their tribal communities, under their own laws. Apart from in the major settlements Maori interaction with the European was minimal.

Grey's contention that 'both races already form one harmonious community, connected together by agricultural and commercial pursuits; professing the same faith, resorting to the same Courts of Justice, joining in the same public sports, standing mutually and indifferently to each other in the relation of landlord and tenant and thus insensibly forming one people', was overly optimistic. By the late 1850s it was evident that a crisis was approaching. The greater demand for land was matched by the growth and organisation of Maori resistance to further land sales. North Island Maoris buried their tribal differences and held numerous multi-tribal meetings in an attempt to co-ordinate resistance to land sales.

The two races were beginning to constitute two nations. In April 1854, about the same time as the General Assembly met in Auckland, about one thousand Maoris gathered at Mana-wapou in Taranaki to discuss the loss of their land. This was the first of a series of great inter-tribal meetings that created a Maori national movement and led to the eventual election of a Maori king. At this first great meeting, the Maoris declared that their remaining lands were tapu: 'The guardians of these lands are bush lawyers, nettles ... tree ferns, reptiles, weta, spiders, taniwha, great lizards.' The first meeting was muddled; there was no cohesiveness and no one leader to unify the tribes in their demands.

Soon the Maori people came to believe that, like the English people, they should have a King — one ruler — and the Maori King Movement was born. The man who did most to mould this movement was chief of the Ngatihaua tribe, Wiremu Tamihana, who became known as the 'Kingmaker'. Tamihana called large meetings in 1857 and 1858 to debate the choosing of a King. His candidate was the great Waikato chief, Potatau Te Wherowhero and his platform was the preservation of lands and a unity of the people. 'The Governor never does anything except when a pakeha is killed,' said

Wiremu Tamihana (also called William Thompson after his baptism), known as the 'Kingmaker'

Tamihana. 'We are allowed to fight and kill each other as we please. A King would end all these evils.'

The debate was furious but in the end, in June 1858, several thousand Maoris recognised Potatau as their King. He had a flag, a council of state, a code of laws, a Resident Magistrate, police and a surveyor. The movement was not merely a copy of the Europeans; the King party wanted to control the type and amount of European influence on their lives. The Maori Kingdom was a fairly loose federation of tribes ranging from the moderate, led by Wiremu Tamihana, to the anti-European extremists led by Rewi, chief of the Ngatimanaipoto tribe. Tribal rivalries were not completely reconciled, but they were united by the resolution to hold on to their land. The Maori tribal system, with the advent of European influence, had begun to fall into decline and the King Movement was a manifestation of the Maoris' desire for law and order amidst the chaotic remains of tribalism. The movement succeeded in arousing much hostility with the settlers and many of them regarded it as a totally treasonable action.

Governor Gore-Browne hoped that by ignoring the movement it would go away: 'I trust that time and absolute indifference, a neglect on the part of the Government, will teach the natives of the folly of proceedings undertaken only by the promptings of vanity and instigated by disappointed advisers.' He planned to avoid any confrontation with the movement and guide it into co-operation with the Government. But the well-meaning Gore-Browne really failed to do anything. He never learned to mix with the Maoris and appointed Donald McLean as the Chief Land Purchase Commissioner and Native Secretary — a bad combination of roles that strengthened the Maoris' belief that the Government's Maori policy was nothing but land purchasing policy. McLean's policy was to ignore the King Movement — he believed they lacked the necessary powers of combination.

Racial relations continued to deteriorate. In 1858 the number of European settlers for the first time was greater than that of the Maoris and mutual resentment over land became critical. There was a growing feeling that war was unavoidable. Gore-Browne in 1859 referred to the vast Maori lands in the North Island — only seven of twenty-six million acres had been purchased — and said, 'the Europeans covet these lands and are determined to enter in and possess them'. Gore-Browne became increasingly hostile towards the Kingites and a clash was inevitable.

Trouble was brewing in Taranaki — an area that represented the most difficult problems of racial relations in the country. From 1854 to 1858 the Province had been in a perpetual uproar of skirmishes and fighting. There were many proposals that the Government should confiscate the lands of Wiremu Kingi and the other chiefs who blocked the land sales. The Provincial Council in 1858 petitioned the Government, urging them to accept proportions of land offered to them by 'friendly' Maoris instead of adhering to the system that required full tribal assent.

The Governor refused this request, but in an effort to maintain law and order announced that any Maoris seen fighting on European land would be treated as rebels. In March 1859, the Governor informed the Maoris that they should sell their land and that he would buy no land unless the owners agreed to sell — *but* he would 'not permit anyone to interfere in the sale of land unless he owned part of it'. Immediately after this speech was read a Maori called Teira offered to sell land at the mouth of the Waitara. The Governor accepted the offer provided a good title could be made out. Wiremu Kingi, principal chief of the Waitara, strongly objected: 'Listen, Governor! Notwithstanding Teira's offer, I will not permit sale of the Wai-

Waitara

108

tara to the pakeha. Waitara is in my hands. I will not give it up — never, never, never! I have spoken.' Whereupon he stormed off in a huff.

By January 1860, Mr Parris, the district land purchaser, had decided that Teira's title was valid and the sale was completed — little attention had been paid to the right of a chief in land sales and the fact that the land had belonged to a tribe as a whole and not merely to the hereditary occupants. On the day of the survey, Kingi sent some old women to pull out the surveyor's pegs. Ten days later martial law was declared. Troops moved in and in retaliation Kingi's men built a pa on the disputed land.

The Governor replied: 'To the chief who obstructs the Queen's road. You have presumed to block up the Queen's road, to build on the Queen's land, and to stop the free passage of persons coming or going. This is levying war against the Queen. Destroy the places you have built; ask my forgiveness, and you shall receive it. If you refuse, the blood of your people be on your own head. I shall fire upon you in twenty minutes from this time if you have not obeyed my order.'

The natives evacuated the pa and the troops destroyed it. Thus began a war. In November 1860 Kingi wrote to a chieftainess: 'peace will not be made, I will continue to fight and the pakehas will be exterminated by me, by my younger brother Te Hapurona . . . it is well with your children and us, we die upon the land which you and your brothers left to us . . . We are here eating the English bullets — My friends, my parents this shall be my work forever. What though my people and I may die, we die for New Zealand.'

On the other side of the coin, Gore-Browne's wife noted in her *Narrative of the Waitara Purchase*: 'Two suns cannot shine in one sky, two kings cannot reign in one dominion and two races cannot avoid collision when living in one country under different laws and yielding obedience to distinct authorities.'

The Maori people would eventually have to submit to the Queen's authority, but for a long time they had it all their own way. They were born to fighting and they knew the terrain. The settlers abandoned their homesteads and took refuge in the small town of New Plymouth, the troops followed them and the Maoris ravaged the surrounding countryside. The Maori King sanctioned the battle saying that Taranaki had been opened 'as a fighting ground for Maoris and pakehas'. Kingi, previously holding aloof from the King Movement now sanctioned it. Tribes from southern Taranaki and large war parties from the Waikato joined Kingi's fifteen hundred rebels and the conflict assumed dangerous proportions.

It was some time before the three thousand European troops became an effective fighting force. The first commander, Colonel Gold, was an inept leader and it was not until he was succeeded by General Pratt that the European's tactics against the Maori's basically defensive method of fighting appeared successful. After a year's manoeuvring and a few battles a truce was called and Kingi retreated to the Waikato. The original dispute was again investigated and Waitara was in time returned to the natives. But feeling still ran high — the war was by no means over and the centre of attention shifted to the Waikato.

Potatau had died in 1860 and his successor, King Tawhiao, was winning increased allegiance amongst the Maoris who were convinced the settlers were going to take their land by force. Gore-Browne wanted to take the offensive. He strongly condemned the King Movement and wished to invade the Waikato before the Kingites went on the warpath. Both the New Zealand General Assembly and the Colonial Office vetoed this prospect, deciding that there were not enough troops to defend the settlements. The British authorities became alarmed at Gore-Browne's aggressive attitude towards the Maoris and decided to send Sir George Grey back to New Zealand as Governor. Before he arrived, McLean resigned and the Stafford ministry lost office. Grey and the new Premier, William Fox, attempted to defuse the Maori situation by introducing a new system of Maori government — Maori assemblies in the various districts were to recommend to the Governor the laws that they required. To no avail — the Kingites now had a deep-rooted suspicion of Government intentions. Grey's problem was two-fold: he had to attempt to maintain the peace and also be prepared if war should break out. As a defensive move he built a road from Auckland to the Waikato, to enable

Attack on the Maori pa at Rangiriri

troop movement in the event of war. The Kingites naturally interpreted this as a forewarning of European attack. All this time the Ngatiruanui tribe had been in armed occupation of a block of Government land at Tataraimaka, south of New Plymouth and they were resolved to hold on to it until Waitara had been returned.

They informed the Governor that if he tried to occupy Tataraimaka without returning Waitara, they would fight. Grey resolved upon decisive action and in April 1863 he and his troops took possession of Tataraimaka. They then began the new investigation of Waitara and decided to return the land to the Maoris — but he was too late — the Maoris acted and in May a small party of soldiers were ambushed near Tataraimaka. Grey defeated these Taranaki rebels, took his troops to Auckland and invaded

the Waikato. The Maoris would not accept his will, so he would have to inflict it. He was deliberately provoking the Waikato Maoris into war to break their military power and seize their most valuable lands.

At dawn on 12 July 1863 British soldiers camped on the Koheroa ridge near the Waikato River and the war began. Lieutenant-General Cameron commanded about eight thousand soldiers and this force was significantly swelled by New Zealand settlers and military settlers hastily recruited in Australia and formed into three companies of 'Waikato Militia'. The most famous commander of the New Zealand settlers was the flamboyant Gustavus Von Tempsky who was highly skilled in guerilla tactics. Against this force the Waikato tribes could muster about six thousand armed men, but not more than one thousand for any one action.

110

General Cameron

Despite Cameron's superiority in numbers and firearms, fighting was difficult. The Maoris normally chose to stand on the defensive in their well-defended pas and Cameron was forced to the offensive throughout the campaign.

The first major action was the attack on Rangiriri. British losses were heavy, thirty-seven dead and ninety-three wounded but the Waikato loss was worse — thirty-six dead were found, one hundred and eighty-three prisoners were taken. Total Maori casualties were at least half the garrison of five hundred. On 8 December Cameron captured the Maori King's capital at Ngaruawahia virtually unopposed and pushed up the Waipa River.

In March he bypassed Paterangi, the most formidable of the pas, occupied Te Awamutu unopposed and pushed on to Rangiaowhia where, against incredible odds, a handful of Maoris refused to surrender. Cameron withdrew, but the next day drove them off in great confusion.

The King Maoris, under Rewi Maniapoto, made their last stand at a village called Orakau. Here they built a pa — not three miles from Cameron's position, it was a direct invitation to fight. For three days, three hundred Maoris were besieged by two thousand troops. The official British report reads: 'They had already been more than two days without water; they had no food but some raw potatoes; an overwhelming force surrounded them, and all hope of relief failed.'

The General took pity on them and asked them to surrender: 'Friends, hear the word of the General. Cease your fighting, you will be taken care of and your lives spared. We have seen your courage; let the fighting stop.' Instantly, an old tattooed chief mounted the breastwork and in a clear ringing voice shouted the intrepid reply: 'Friends, this is the reply of the Maori. We shall fight on, *ake, ake, ake* [forever, forever, forever].' 'If you are determined to die,' replied the General, 'give up your women and children and we will take care of them.' The defiant answer was: 'Who is it that is to die? Wait a little: our women also fight.' On the afternoon of the third day the Maoris charged out in a body. Amidst the confusion about half of the Maoris escaped into the swamps and the other half died.

The Waikato had fallen — the whole of the Waikato lowlands was under military occupation, its Maori owners either dead or expelled. But the greater Maori losses, the confiscation of land and the unjustified invasion, were not to be forgotten.

Large groups of Maoris from Tauranga in the Bay of Plenty had assisted in the Taranaki war and Cameron, wanting to tie all loose

The attack to the Orakau pa

Incident at the Gate pa

knots, sent an expedition to quell them. The Maoris scored a notable victory at Gate Pa but were eventually overwhelmed at Te Ranga.

By 1864 the main tribes of the King Movement were defeated. Only Taranaki remained. And a new threat had arisen in this volatile Province: the Good and Peaceful Religion. In 1862 the Angel Gabriel had appeared to the Maori Te Ua and this Maori who had fought in the Taranaki Wars founded a new faith, a curious jumble of Christianity, Judaism and paganism. One of the major tenets of this faith was invulnerability in battle, created by the utterance of the magical word 'Hau'. His followers became known as Hauhaus and they believed they were a Chosen people and with divine aid they would return from the wilderness to their hereditary lands.

The movement gained many supporters amongst the disgruntled Maoris and the fighting that resulted in the Taranaki and East Cape

was the fiercest and most savage of all the campaigns. Believing themselves invincible the Hauhaus fought quite recklessly against the often hopeless odds. Hauhauism was a somewhat fanatical resort of a people driven to despair; yet it gave them a belief in the success of their cause which objectively seemed hopeless. By 1866 Te Ua had been captured and renounced his beliefs and much of his following died away; but his teachings were to be revived in a different form as the Ringatu faith devised by the Maori warrior Te Kooti.

Meanwhile the European was having other problems. In 1862 the Crown monopoly of the purchase of Maori land was abolished and 'free trade' allowed. In 1863 Grey had suggested that the Government should punish the rebels by confiscating their lands and a year later saw a bitter quarrel between Grey and his ministers as to which land should be confiscated.

Nearly three million acres were eventually confiscated in the Waikato, on the East Coast and in Taranaki and this land was confiscated unfairly. The Government took prime land,

A typical siege during the Maori wars

112

whether it belonged to rebels or to tribes who had played little part in the fighting. It was a terrible injustice and embittered relations with the Maoris for generations.

Problems also arose between the British Government who expected their troops in New Zealand to have some say in Maori affairs and the General Assembly who in 1863 had been given the responsibility for administering native affairs. The British Government felt the only solution was to withdraw their troops and let the colonists control Maori policy and fight their own wars. In 1865 and 1866 all but one of the regiments sailed back to Great Britain.

In 1868 Grey was dismissed and in 1870 the last regiment withdrawn from New Zealand. The colonists were on their own. Bitter fighting, sieges and skirmishes still disturbed Taranaki and the East Coast. In 1868 the rebels found themselves a new leader, Te Kooti, who escaped from captivity on the Chatham Islands to conduct a brilliant guerilla warfare campaign from his Urewera sanctuary until, with the participants exhausted, fighting petered out in 1872. Te Kooti founded a new religion — Ringatu, a Maori variant of Christianity retaining some of the paganism of the Hauhau cult. He also began a series of raids and massacres upon the Poverty Bay settlers — loyal natives and Europeans being killed alike. Chased by both settlers and friendly Maoris he was eventually hounded into the King country where he found sanctuary.

The wars drew to an end but it was not until the 1880s when King Tawhiao made his peace with the Government and Te Kooti was finally pardoned that the white man dared enter the King Country — a brooding ground for many of the sullen exiled Maoris. The *Picturesque Atlas of Australasia* solemnly recounts:

The situation in 1888 is one of profound and settled repose; the Queen's writ runs uninterruptedly through the length and breadth of the colony and there is every assurance for the hope that native wars in New Zealand are at an end. In 1879 Rewi, the hero of Orakau, visited Auckland for the first time in twenty years, and was lionised by the citizens. He returned to the Waikato in company with the Governor, Sir Hercules Robinson,

Rewi Mani Poto

deeply impressed with the marvels wrought by the all-subduing pakeha. Early in 1882 Tawhiao, the King, came forth from his seclusion and also visited Auckland, where all sorts of honours were lavished on him. He subsequently visited England and is now living quietly in his home in the Waikato. At the beginning of 1888 he held a meeting at Maungakawa at the invitation of the Ngatihaua tribe, when the following lines of policy were affirmed: 'That the Maoris and pakehas shall be as one people; obey the laws of the Queen, and respect them in every way as loyal subjects; and that every native acting contrary to the Queen's laws shall undergo the same punishment as the pakeha; that all natives avoid intoxication and other abuses; that no objection be offered to the Native Lands Court selling or otherwise so long as it is done legally.' With this declaration the long dispute between the two races, which had lasted from the very beginning of colonisation, at last came to an end.

Active and passive resistance had failed but it was many years until the smouldering resentment subsided. The Land Wars had unlocked the Maori land — by 1892 a total 6.8 million hectares of Maori land had been either confiscated or sold; they were left with 4.4 million hectares, much of it unusable. The land laws became to the Maori a jungle of confusion and their will to resist had been broken. They had fought extremely bravely for their heritage — the British army historian J. W. Fortescue wrote that the British soldier found the Maoris 'on the whole the grandest enemy that he had ever encountered'. But it was to no avail.

Gold fever

The Maori wars were not the only dramatic events of the 1800s. Gold fever spread through New Zealand like a contagious disease during this period. The Californian and Australian fields were in their heyday in the mid-1800s and many New Zealanders were heading for the Australian fields. Alarmed at this exodus some Auckland businessmen offered a £500 reward to anyone who discovered a payable goldfield in the top half of the North Island. And in 1852, Charles Ring, a sawmiller at Coromandel and experienced prospector on the Californian goldfields struck gold on the banks of a stream running from the foot of the Tokatea Range into the Coromandel Harbour. Gold had been discovered in New Zealand.

The Coromandel and Thames diggings
Within a month three hundred diggers moved into the area. Forty-one square kilometres were immediately leased for three years from local Maoris and licences issued at thirty shillings a month. The New Zealand gold rush was underway. But the first of these rushes was to be doomed to peter out with less than £1500 worth of gold to show for it. The prospectors soon exhausted the beds of the Waiau and Matawai streams. The real wealth of Coromandel, the quartz deposits, still lay undiscovered. The Maori Wars were also a contributing factor to the dwindling of this first Coromandel goldfield — the miners became unsettled by the fighting and many of them headed for the more lucrative goldfields of the South Island. However, in 1862 Coromandel was again proclaimed a goldfield. Geologists had recognised the existence of exploitable quartz fields and boundary negotiations resumed with the local tribes. But only small windfalls of gold were found in the area and attention shifted to the quartz fields in Thames. A series of delicate negotiations with local Maoris resulted in the proclamation of Thames as a goldfield in July 1867.

At first the miners were disgruntled as the area did not appear to be rich in gold. But on 10 August W. A. Hunt discovered the fabulous 'Shotover' on the Kuranui Stream and the stampede to the Thames area began. The town of Thames sprang up and within three years had a population of twenty thousand, twice the size of Auckland. It was a raw, rumbustious town with few public facilities and over one hundred hotels. Amazing finds came quickly — the 'Golden Crown', 'Manukau' and 'Caledonian' — but the alluvial gold was quickly exhausted and the expense of working quartz claims proved too costly for the individual miners who gave way to larger companies. Nearly £2 million of gold was produced in 1871 when over seventy mines were working but the output steadily declined and only negligible amounts were recorded from 1912 on. Thames yielded £7 178 000 between 1867 and 1924.

Breakfast on the goldfields

114

The Otago diggings

The flow of yellow wealth extended southwards. While the land wars were occupying the North Island settlers, gold tipped the balance in favour of the South and miners flooded in. On 23 May 1861 Gabriel Read struck gold in what was to be known as Gabriel's Gully. He wrote: 'At a place where a kind of road crossed on a shallow bar I shovelled away about two and a half feet of gravel, arrived at a beautiful soft slate and saw the gold shining like the stars in Orion on a dark frosty night. It was dark ere I have finished properly washing this prospect. I had got deeply interested in my work...'. He immediately made public his find and ushered in a whole change in the pattern of life in Otago. Read's find galvanised Dunedin and the rush to Tuapeka started.

On 6 July 1816 the editor of the *Otago Witness* wrote:

Gold, gold, gold is the universal subject of conversation.... The number of persons leaving town each morning is quite surprising. The fever is running at such a height that, if it continues, there will scarcely be a man left in the town.... The Tokomairiro plain is positively deserted. Master and man have gone together on equal terms, leaving their farming arrangements under an agreement to return to reap crops; but, if the fever continues, there will be little crop, we should think, to reap. The men having left the plain, there appeared no remedy; and we are informed that the women and children in numberless cases have gone also. On the last Sunday the congregation at church consisted of the Minister and precentor.

A few months later Horatio Hartley and Christopher Reilly stunned Dunedin by their 8716 bags of gold from what became known as the Dunstan diggings. The gold had come from the Clutha River. This discovery completely overshadowed Gabriel Read's and men poured into the district from Tuapeka, Dunedin and all over New Zealand and Australia. The *Otago Daily Times* wrote:

Money seems almost as plentiful as in the old days in Victoria. The diggings are turning out beyond the most sanguine expectations.... The district is opening up so rapidly that the very mention of names is bewildering. Gold is found everywhere and there is room enough for thousands. As a summer diggings the surrounding country is proving itself capable to maintain all who come and only requires to be tested to unfold its vast resources and its enormous wealth.... It is an impossibility not to speak in too glowing terms of the value of the Dunstan goldfields. As a winter diggings the Molyneaux [Clutha], the Kawarau, the Manuherikia and their many tributaries will employ a population that must eventually be counted by tens of thousands.... No goldfield in any portion of the world offers so great a variety of diggings as this. Rivers, creeks, flats, gullies everywhere present themselves and the labour required is of the easiest kind. When heavy gold, like that at Cardrona, can be picked upon the surface, and the average depth of the surface does not exceed six feet, and in creeks none at all, the natural advantage it thus possesses renders any competition with it out of the question. The Lachlan, British Columbia, the goldfields of Victoria have shown nothing equal to this in extent of resources, and it is thought by many the lower workings will eclipse in richness all previous discoveries....

Then came the even more sensational Wakatipu goldfield. The remote Shotover River proved to be incredibly rich in gold and this discovery led to the greatest gold rush in Otago's history. Mining communities spread rapidly — to Arrowtown, Queenstown and many others scattered along the river. There was gold in almost every river in Wakatipu. People flocked to Dunedin from all over the world and Dunedin's economy boomed as never before or since. It was transformed from a village to the foremost town in New Zealand and earned itself the title of 'commercial capital of New Zealand'.

The West Coast diggings

The Otago riches for a time overshadowed the finds on the West Coast but once the initial finds began to dwindle many miners crossed

The head of Lake Wakatipu

the Alps, tempted by reports of rich finds to the west. The largely uninhabited West Coast had been summarily dismissed by most explorers and settlers but in 1866 about sixteen thousand miners were swelling the population ranks. Gold had initiated colonisation of this rugged area. The area had previously been famous for a different kind of wealth — greenstone — and many Maoris had trekked out in search of the precious stone. Early in January 1864, two Maoris in the process of removing a block of greenstone on the main branch of the Hohonu River found coarse gold.

Further discoveries were made and by the end of the year 1400 ounces of gold had been won and the towns of Greymouth and Hokitika had begun to take shape. Then came the big rushes to the fields of Waimea, Kaniere and Ross. Miners poured into the area, six thousand arriving in March 1865 alone and then the Australian invasion began. By the close of the year about five thousand men had disembarked at

Hokitika from Australia. From 1865 to 1867 gold worth over £5 million was exported from the West Coast. Hokitika's growth was phenomenal — in 1867 more overseas vessels called at Hokitika than at any other port in New Zealand and between the years 1865 and 1867 approximately thirty-seven thousand migrants crossed the Hokitika bar. In 1867, with a population of four thousand six hundred and eighty-eight it was New Zealand's sixth largest town. Gold had carved a living community out of the West Coast's bush. But the boom waned as suddenly as it had begun. The last real rush was in May 1867 to Addisons Flat near Westport. Many prospectors left for the newly proclaimed fields in Coromandel. But until 1895, the West Coast remained the country's chief gold-producing region.

Gold brought many things to New Zealand — an influx of settlers, a rapid rise in the economy and an opening up of the South Island — but perhaps most of all it brought hope and

116

The port of Greymouth

excitement at a time when the country was beset with land problems and the Maori wars.

Pastoralism and social reform

Gold created an illusion of prosperity in New Zealand in the 1860s and for a decade it accounted for more than half of the country's income. But when the gold was nearly exhausted New Zealand again had to face the problem of building an economy in a land that lacked mineral resources and it became apparent that New Zealand would have to rely upon pastoral farming.

The 1850s to the 1880s were known as the 'wool period'. After gold, wool was the country's major export and in 1870 it accounted for half the country's income. Early sheep farming was an extremely hard life — the settlers had a heavy task breaking in their land. 'It is rather rough work at first in the bush', said one early Taranaki settler, 'you have to make yourself a small hut of poles and thatch ... light a good fire in the middle and at night roll yourself up in your blankets, then, possessing a contented mind, you fall asleep and dream of the days when the mighty forest will have given away before the axe and the fire to beautiful green fields ... and you wake on the morrow with fresh strength to do your share in the glorious work ... of subduing and replenishing the earth.'

Gradually pastoralism spread. In 1843 some Wellington settlers rented Wairarapa Maori land for sheep farming. Charles Bidwill in 1844 with a flock of three hundred and fifty was the first sheepman in the Wairarapa. In 1847 a sheep station was set up in the Marlborough district and as early as 1843 some enterprising settlers were raising sheep on Banks Peninsula and the Canterbury Plains. By the time the Pilgrims arrived in Canterbury in 1850 the Deans brothers on their four hundred acres at Riccarton were offering a fine example of sheep farming and before the settlement at Christchurch had celebrated its second anniversary the age of pastoralism had dawned. Before the end of Canterbury's first decade sheep numbers had reached three-quarters of a million and the region was almost wholly occupied by sheepmen.

At home

117

Though few in numbers, the great run-holders formed a political, economic and social ruling class. Sheep farmers obtained from the Crown the use of large areas of land and some security of tenure. The sheep cost about £1 each and shepherds were employed for about £60 a year. These runholders, usually men of capital, controlled most of the wealth of the country and by the early 1860s occupied almost all the open country on the east coast of both the North and South Islands. Most of the large runs — above fifty thousand acres — were in Marlborough, Otago and Canterbury. Otago contained nineteen holdings of over one hundred thousand acres, Canterbury four and no other district more than one. Robert Campbell was the doyen of the sheep kings in Otago — he had properties holding three hundred thousand sheep. By comparison the Canterbury runs were rather small and had fewer flocks of more than twenty thousand sheep.

Shearing

These mighty pastoralists held great influence in Council and Parliament. It was generally recognised that the prosperity of New Zealand depended on their production of wool. There were at any one time less than two hundred runholders in Canterbury and from their ranks came more than a quarter of the Provincial Councillors. The sheep men were the 'squattocracy' of New Zealand.

The small farmers, the agriculturalists, began to vie with these 'big men' for space on the more arable lands. The system of 'free selection' enabled small farmers to choose land available for selection and buy the freehold. The runholders had to exercise their pre-emptive rights and freehold parts of their leaseholds or else lose them. To defend their holdings runholders would often indulge in 'grid-ironing' or 'spotting' — strategically freeholding key areas such as the homestead block, making it quite impracticable for anyone to try and farm the remaining areas by themselves.

Julius Vogel was the man who gave the small farmer his chance. By the end of the 1860s the price of wool was down in Canterbury and the runs were in many cases overstocked as grazing land had been diminished by the rabbit invasion. By 1868 surplus sheep had become unsaleable and farmers often drove their unwanted sheep over cliffs until the practice of boiling-down carcasses for tallow reduced the waste.

Business was almost at a standstill in the towns — particularly in the north where the costly Maori wars had slowed the economy and depleted the Government's funds. Into this depressing arena came Vogel, a man with remarkable political talents who was in 1870 Treasurer of the ministry led by William Fox. Vogel reasoned that the way out of a slump was to inject borrowed money into the economy, setting aside public land for sale in order to repay the loans. He was faced with one major stumbling block — the provincial governments who controlled the disposal of land opposed his scheme. Undeterred, Vogel, when he became Premier in 1874, launched the legislation that abolished the Provinces. Even though his borrowing scheme was initially stripped of safeguards, Vogel pressed ahead and between 1870 and 1880, £20 million were borrowed. Railways, roads, bridges and government buildings were constructed and the population doubled. The colony had gained thousands of useful settlers and many essential public works. The boom had arrived.

Land values were pushed up by the improved transport and the great profits of both wheat and improved sheep farming. Canterbury had an agricultural bonanza — four hundred thousand acres of tussock land was ploughed and turned and speculation in land reached a fever pitch. By 1878 nearly all the plains had been freeholded by small farmers or the wealthier former leaseholders.

Land prices were high — £2 an acre — but this was no deterrent. Although improved by the buoyant economy, circumstances were, however, not totally favourable to the under-capitalised small farmer. In 1883 47 per cent of the two million eight hundred thousand acres sold in Canterbury was still controlled by only ninety-one persons.

The agricultural boom was further boosted by the advent of refrigeration. Runs were overstocked and the demand for surplus meat was limited. Refrigeration brought the meat-hungry markets of Britain within easy reach and the steamship *Dunedin* took the first cargo of meat from New Zealand to England in 1882. A new era for New Zealand primary production was heralded and within ten years annual exports reached 1.9 million carcasses. Prices were only about threepence a pound but the sales enabled the sheep industry to expand. The end of the 'wool period' arrived and emphasis was placed on meat production.

Borrowed wealth had created a few years of excitement and progress in New Zealand but by 1879 trouble was brewing. Wheat and wool prices had already begun to fall and bankers contracted credit facilities in New Zealand. A slump began and land speculation came to a halt. Wrote one historian: 'Few extensive holdings were being worked to anything like the best advantage... many were in the grip of the financiers, and were carried on from year to year with the least possible outlay of capital. It was commonplace that half the great estates were for sale; and so they were, at a price. The mortgagees would not sell at a loss, and could seldom sell at a profit. They hung on to the land

watching one another and waiting for a rise in prices and for a brisk demand which naturally did not come. And, whilst the country was just fitted for working farmers, and lying empty and waiting for their hands, men in hundreds and thousands, farmers' sons and country labourers, were growing up and working on other men's land, albeit they had the skill, knowledge and strength to manage the holdings on their own. The cry for land in New Zealand in 1890 was no mere urban sentimentalism....'

Canterbury, which had probably benefited most from Vogel's boom period, felt the depression the heaviest. Runholders lost their properties to banks and many small farmers were forced off the land back into town where the ranks of the unemployed swelled. Many thousands left New Zealand. Something had to be done to change New Zealand's economy and slowly, with the aid of changing technology, a vital new industry — dairy farming — developed that consolidated the country's agricultural economy and enabled the small farmer to confidently join the arena.

Politics also played a major part in farm development. A new order had emerged out of the depression that had lasted from 1879 to 1896. In 1890 the Liberal Party under John Ballance came to power with policies pledged to closer settlement by the repurchase of the large estates for subdivision by the Crown, the

Queen's Wharf; loading frozen mutton

imposition of a land tax to try to force voluntary subdivision of large holdings and cheap finance for new farm development. Between 1891 and 1911 the area of land owned privately in estates of over 4000 hectares was reduced from 2.8 million to 1.2 million hectares and the number of individual holdings increased from less than 44 000 to nearly 74 000.

The Liberals created over 5000 new farms and let them to approved applicants. The growing dairy industry in the North Island was luring many farmers away from the South and the pastoral economy spread throughout New Zealand. The old order came to an end. The dominance of the early colonial gentry with their monopoly of sheep runs had been shattered with the advent of the Liberal Government and a democracy was in power. The Liberals held power until 1912, first under Ballance and later under Richard Seddon. It was a period of great democratic and humanitarian legislation. New Zealand led the world in social reform; the vote was extended to women, compulsory state arbitration in industrial disputes was introduced and the first Old Age Pension scheme was established.

The Liberals' success in blending capitalism with socialism earned for New Zealand the modern description of being 'the birthplace of the twentieth century'. The English statesman, Asquith, described New Zealand as 'a laboratory in which political and social experiments are every day made for the information and instruction of the older countries of the world'. Seddon died in 1906. The Liberal Party gradually lost touch with the people and the Labour movement broke away and formed its own independent party. The election of the Liberal Government in 1890 had led to the organisation of a conservative opposition — the Reform Party — which was backed by business and large landowners. In the 1930s the remnants of the Reform and old Liberal parties united to form the National Party and Labour and National have alternated as Governments since 1935. Today, these two major parties both lay claim to being Seddon's political heirs.

New Zealand today still relies on its primary industries, agriculture providing more than 80 per cent of the country's export income. Of the country's total area of about 27 million hectares, 14 million are devoted to farming. The importance of agriculture influences most of the industrial work in New Zealand which involves the processing of agricultural products. Close ties with Britain have been weakened and New Zealand now has a newly defined identity as an Asian-Pacific nation. The European heritage remains but is modified by the existence of some 270000 Maoris and 80000 Polynesians. There is a strong awareness of a multi-cultural, multi-racial identity. New Zealand is a unique land where early struggles and hardships have fashioned an independent spirit. New Zealanders today are the true inheritors of a dream.

Hop-picking near Nelson

120

Picton, gateway to the South Island. (Kleinpaste)

Opposite, above and below: *The Marlborough Sounds, an interlocking jigsaw of land and water. (Fairlie, Kleinpaste)*

Below: *Yachts stretch their masts into the sky at Nelson. Named after Lord Nelson, this sunny city was the second of Edward Gibbon Wakefield's New Zealand Company Settlements. (Prenzel)*

Overleaf: *Rich pastoral land of the Motueka Valley, near Nelson. (Kendall)*

Top: *The Richmond Ranges tower over the sheep-studded plains of the Wairau Valley. (Kendall)*

Centre: *The Hope River — one of the many rivers dissecting the rocky peaks and forest areas of the north-west corner of the South Island. (Collinson)*

Bottom: *Forests of black and red beech creep down to the shores of Lake Rotoiti which covers nearly 1000 hectares of the Nelson Lakes National Park. (Collinson)*

Opposite, above left: *The slender, beech-fringed glacial Lake Rotoroa, popular for brown trout. (Kleinpaste)*

Opposite, above right and bottom: *The Kaikoura Ranges, reaching 2885 metres, contrast towering snowy mountains with placid sheep runs. (Kendall)*

The Seaward Kaikoura Range dwarfs the township of Kaikoura. Kaikoura is Maori for 'to eat crayfish' and crayfishing plays a large part in this area's economy. (Prenzel)

The Buller River on one of its gentler stretches near Murchison. (Collinson)

The eroded limestone formation of the Pancake Rocks at Punakaiki. (Kleinpaste)

The Inangahua River — inanga is the Maori word for whitebait, a delicacy caught on its return migration from sea to river. (Kendall)

Above left: *Cliff-bound beaches of the 88 608-hectare Westland National Park where spurs of high ranges reach into the sea.* (Kendall)

Above: *Shantytown — the historical reproduction of an early gold mining town.* (Kendall)

Right: *Port of the surrounding coal mining and saw-milling district, Greymouth is the largest town on the West Coast.* (Collinson)

Left: *The golden blooms of the kowhai, one of the country's best known natives.* (Kleinpaste)

Left and below: *The Fox and Franz Joseph Glaciers slide spectacularly into the Westland forest. The fractured pattern of ice is caused by the centre of the glacier flowing faster than the sides. (Kendall, Collinson)*

Opposite: *Mt Tasman in the Westland National Park. (Kendall)*

Bottom: *Deposits left by vanished glaciers in Westland. (Collinson)*

The milky waters of Lake Pukaki provide a perfect foreground for the country's tallest peak — Mt Cook. (Kleinpaste)

Opposite: *A ski plane perches on the Tasman Glacier — at 29 kilometres it is the longest glacier in the country. (Collinson)*

Below: *Seen across the Tasman River, New Zealand's highest mountain, Mt Cook, rises to 3764 metres above sea level. (Collinson)*

135

The Mt Cook lily, Ranunculus lyalli, *the most exquisite of all New Zealand's alpine plants.* (Collinson)

The Maoris call Mt Cook, 'Aorangi', or 'cloud in the sky'. Cook probably never saw this great mountain which was named after him by Captain John Stokes when surveying the West Coast. (Collinson)

One of Mt Cook's neighbours, Mt Sefton (3157 metres), called by the Maoris 'Maunga Atua' — 'mountain of the gods'. (Collinson)

Below: *The Haast River, after being joined by the bigger Landsborough River, runs through a wide valley, surrounded by forest-clad slopes.*

Opposite: Southland rata adorns the banks of the Haast River, Haast Pass. (Kendall)

The fur seal, the only species of seal that breeds on the mainland, found in Westland, Fiordland and Foveaux Strain. (Kleinpaste)

The rugged and bush-clad headland of Knights Point, a sanctuary and feeding ground for seals. (Kendall)

The Wilkin River drains a rugged and spectacular 32-kilometre stretch of the Southern Alps. (Waite)

Gnarled, leached driftwood litters the southern beaches of Westland. (Collinson)

The deep, glistening waters of Lake Wanaka mirror alpine peaks. (Kleinpaste)

Below: *Grassy flats contrast with the rugged mountain peaks of Westland. (Collinson)*

Bottom: *The white-frosted peaks of Mt Aspiring rise behind the Matukituki Valley. (Kendall)*

Overleaf: *The Church of the Good Shepherd stands vigil over the turquoise waters of Lake Tekapo and (inset) the peaks of Mt Cook can be seen through the chancel window. (Kendall, Kleinpaste)*

Inscribed on the base of this momument to the sheep dog are the words: 'This monument was erected by the runholders of the MacKenzie Country and those who also appreciate the value of the collie dog, without the help of which the grazing of this mountain country would be impossible.' (Kendall)

Left: Beech forest lines Lewis Pass, the most northerly east-west pass, named after a Nelson surveyor, Henry Lewis. (Kendall)

Opposite, above: Beautiful Lake Alexandrina in the MacKenzie Country was named after Queen Alexandra. (Kendall)

Opposite, below: Mt Cook provides Lake Pukaki with a backdrop of unparalleled grandeur. (Prenzel)

Below: The sparkling blue of the waters of Lake Tekapo is caused by suspended ground rock which helps reflect the light. (Kendall)

146

Magnificent bush and mountain country surrounding Arthur's Pass, discovered by Arthur Dudley Dobson in 1864. (Kendall)

Right: *Golden wheat harvest near Waiau. (Prenzel)*

Opposite: *The Waiau River near Hanmer Springs — thermal area and tourist resort. (Kendall)*

Overleaf: *Across the entrance to the estuary from the long bar of South New Brighton is the small settlement of Sumner. (Prenzel)*

The Waimakariri River, originating in the Southern Alps, sprawls across the Canterbury Plains on its way to the sea. (Kendall)

Below: *The peaks of the Craigieburn Range are reflected in the tranquil waters of Lake Pearson. (Kendall)*

Opposite: *The copper-sheathed spire of Christchurch Cathedral rises 65.6 metres above Cathedral Square. (Robinson)*

Right and below: *Trees trail their branches into the River Avon which wends its way through the heart of Christchurch, New Zealand's garden city. (Prenzel)*

Men who made New Zealand

Captain James Cook

Behind every country there are great men. Men that have shaped, moulded and set new directions for a burgeoning society. Not all these men — these instigators of change — have had a positive effect. The negative changes also affected the direction New Zealand's early society moved in. Here are some of these people — the good and the bad — who have made New Zealand what it is today.

Captain James Cook

The man who put New Zealand on the map, James Cook, was born to a farm labourer at a Yorkshire hamlet, Marton-in-Cleveland, on 27 October 1728. He received only the merest rudiments of education and was apprenticed to a draper at the age of seventeen. Eighteen months after his appointment the young James

left — he wanted to go to sea. He bound himself apprentice to a coal-carrying barque and by the time he reached his mid-twenties had become a mate. In 1755 war broke out between England and France and press-gangs set out to man His Majesty's ships. Cook made another decision, he joined the Navy as an able seaman, the only rank open to him, and a few weeks after joining the *Eagle* was made Master's Mate. Step-by-step Cook moved upwards. He reached the warrant rank of Master and on his twenty-ninth birthday was appointed to the *Pembroke* on the North America station. Here, it was Cook's task to find a way for ships to sail within range of Quebec's forts. The work was done so well that the chart of the St Lawrence river which grew out of information collected by Cook was used for over one hundred years.

Cook was demonstrating outstanding ability as a pilot and marine surveyor. For five years he charted the hazardous Newfoundland Coast and in 1766 he observed the eclipse of the sun from Newfoundland and sent a paper on his observations to the Royal Society in London. This factor, along with his other skills gave him the reputation in scientific circles of being a man of outstanding ability.

Cook's next great chance to further his career came when the Royal Society petitioned the King to send a ship to observe the 1769 transit of Venus, visible only in the Pacific Ocean. Cook was chosen and on 25 August 1768 he set off for the Pacific in the *Endeavour*. The first of his celebrated voyages had begun. In three voyages of discovery he mapped new parts of the Pacific, destroyed the myth of a great southern continent and sailed around New Zealand, charting its coast. He discovered and charted the east coast of Australia and went deep into the Antarctic. He explored Arctic coasts and uncovered islands and archipelagos below the Equator. His professional ability was outstanding and he showed infinite patience in surveying the coast of the lands he discovered.

He was also a man of great humanity, as shown by his relationship with the native people — especially the Maoris, of whom he said: 'I must ... observe in favour of the New Zealanders that I have always found them of a brave, noble, open and benevolent disposition. But they are a people that will never put up with an insult if they have an opportunity to resent it.' Sadly, it was also the native people that Cook sought so strongly to understand who were responsible for his death. On the fateful morning of 14 February 1779 Cook went ashore at Kealakekua Bay in Hawaii to investigate the theft of a cutter. There was no news of it and Cook resolved to take the King prisoner until the cutter was returned. A large crowd of natives gathered as the King was being led down the shore. Just at this moment, news was brought to the natives that the English had killed a chief on another part of the island. Cook, fearing bloodshed, released the King but it was too late. The natives attacked with a shower of stones and Cook, hit on the head, fell into shallow water and was overcome by a rush of natives who stabbed him to death.

A truly noble character, Cook remains a hero in the annals of New Zealand history for his claiming of the country for the West and for the world.

Samuel Marsden, Henry Williams and Bishop Pompallier — men of God

SAMUEL MARSDEN

Samuel Marsden was the founder of missionary work in New Zealand. Educated by evangelical charity at Magdalene College in Cambridge, he was appointed to the position of chaplain of the penal settlement at New South Wales in 1795. Alienated from his potential congregation by the harsh attitudes he assumed towards the convicts and emancipists, Marsden was not a popular man. He vigorously enforced Old Testament discipline and was known as the 'Flogging Parson' through his free use of the lash for discipline.

Reverend Samuel Marsden

Not entirely happy with his missionary role in New Zealand, Marsden decided to expand his horizons into the foundation of a mission to New Zealand. In 1807 he returned to England and enlisted the aid of the Church Missionary Society in establishing a mission settlement in New Zealand. His plan was to elevate the Maori from their 'degraded state' by teaching them of the material trade skills and trade goods of late eighteenth-century England. By 1814 Marsden was ready to proceed. He had selected three settlers to help him; a carpenter, a twine spinner and a teacher. He informed the Bay of Island settlers of his intentions in a letter written to chief Ruatara: 'Duaterra [sic] King, I have sent the Brig *Active* to the Bay of Islands to see what you are doing; and Mr Hall and Mr Kendall from England.... You will be very good to Mr Hall and Mr Kendall. They will come to live in New Zealand if you will not hurt them; and teach you how to grow corn, wheat and make houses and every thing.'

In November he sailed for New Zealand and chose Rangihoua in the northern part of the Bay of Islands as his mission site. On 24 February the following year he returned to New South Wales, leaving Hall, Kendall and King in charge.

Marsden, as Agent of the Church Missionary Society, was meant to form a committee to assist him in operating the settlement, but he chose to retain absolute control. It was a difficult situation for Kendall and the others. 'Mr Marsden will have his way in everything,' wrote Kendall, 'he pays little regard to the opinion of others yet is the most slovenly man for a pious man I almost ever heard of ... he pays no attention to arrangement or system nor does he gain the good will of those with whom he has to deal.'

Kendall thought Marsden both dictatorial and parsimonious. The Maori school failed because Marsden failed to provide adequate food supplies upon which attendance depended. At the heart of the conflict was the fact that there were not enough supplies and yet Marsden refused to accept the settlers' views that produce could not be purchased from the Maoris without using arms for barter. He did, however, fail to stop the trade in arms, admitting that 'in every part of New Zealand' he had been charged 'by the Natives ... with sending Missionaries to the Bay of Islands who put muskets into the hands of their Enemies to kill them — these charges I could not deny'.

Marsden made seven visits to the New Zealand mission between 1814 and 1837. Each time he hammered out rules and agreements and each time conflicts again broke out when he returned to New South Wales. As Kendall said in a letter to Marsden: 'I think you expect too much from measures of a temporal nature. You seem to give more encouragement to husbandry and agriculture and to be more zealous respecting them than you are about churches and schools.'

Much conflict surrounded Marsden's estab-lishment of the mission. But his dedication to the conversion of the Maoris was unquestion-able and throughout his life he did much to protect them from ill-treatment and fraudulent dealings. His righteousness limited early success but his claim to fame remains as the 'founding father' of the missionary movement in New Zealand.

JOHN WILLIÁMS

The leadership and practical ability which the early Anglican mission so badly needed was found in the person of Henry Williams. The early years of the mission were surrounded by personal bickering and their position was ex-tremely dependent on Maori tolerance and their own willingness to trade in muskets; the latter being about the only aspect of European civilisation that the Maori was interested in.

The arrival of Henry Williams in 1823 was an important factor in the success of missionary work. Born in Nottingham, England, in 1792 Williams had a chequered career first in the Navy and then as a drawing master. In 1818 he became interested in mission work which cul-minated in his arrival in the Bay of Islands in August 1823. Here he dismissed Kendall, who was having a liaison with a Maori woman, and Butler, an alleged drunk, and as the only re-maining ordained man he assumed leadership of the mission. His influence on mission policy was to guide the adoption of the translation of the Bible into Maori and the teaching of it in schools. This policy bore fruit as the Maoris became attracted to Christianity by their inter-est in mastering the skills of literacy. The mission's work thus shifted its emphasis from practical skills to teaching.

In the 1830s Williams set off to expand beyond the Bay of Islands and establish stations in the southern part of the North Island. And with the help of the translated religious works Christianity began to spread.

Williams' leadership soon gained respect from the Maoris and they began to enlist his aid as mediator in tribal disputes. He did much to ease the Maoris' change to a new way of life when it was desirable that they should put an end to tribal warfare.

However, his role as a peacemaker was to be part of Williams' downfall. When war broke out in the north in 1845, Williams did all he could to try and help make peace between the two parties and was called a traitor by one British officer. Governor Grey, in an attempt to break the missionaries' influence took up a charge of treachery against Williams. Gaining little support by using these allegations, Grey then turned to a more damaging charge and asserted that the missionaries' land claims had been the main cause of the Maori wars. Williams refuted the charges but the Church Mission Society in England, upset at the conflict between missionaries and government, dismissed Williams in 1849.

Williams was a strong, determined leader who introduced cohesion into the early mission days. The change in mission policy had been made before his arrival but his contribution was the ability to carry out the new policy.

BISHOP POMPALLIER

The foundations of the Catholic Church in New Zealand were laid by Bishop Pompallier. Born at Lyons, France, on 11 December 1801, the son of a wealthy silk merchant, he began his studies for the priesthood in 1825 and was ordained in 1829. Pompallier arrived at Hokianga on 10 January 1838 and so began long years of antagonism between Catholic and Protestant missions. Although arriving many years after their rivals, the Catholics did enjoy a limited success with the Maoris: many tribes rejected the Protestants as they did not want to join the same mission as rival tribes. But a shortage of funds and the disturbed patterns of race relations in nineteenth-century New Zealand made the going difficult.

Pompallier had succeeded in stimulating the interest of Catholicism over a wide area — missionaries were posted from North Auckland to the Bay of Plenty — but there were insufficient priests to follow up this interest. Also the ones that did exist were not respected by the Maoris because of their extreme poverty. In 1846 Pompallier reported that about five thousand Maoris had been baptised and about five times that number could be considered converts. But his methods were not forceful enough. Father Jean Forest wrote in 1842:

His heart is too kind. He can refuse no one.

At times not having any money he borrows . . . to buy clothes for the Maoris he is going to visit. . . . Here is how the 'conversions' are effected that we read about: the Bishop would go through the tribes with a certain amount of clothing. The natives would flock around him to get a dress or handkerchief declaring 'I am a *picopo* [Catholic].' At these words the Bishop believed conversions made. He instructed them in a few days, baptised several of them and left them with the promise of a priest who never came, so that the natives turned into Protestants saying that the Catholic bishop was a liar.

Pompallier's area of control was gradually reduced and in 1848 the Marists were sent to work under a new Bishop in a new diocese in Wellington. Pompallier remained in Auckland and in 1850 brought eight Sisters of Mercy to the city to open schools for both Maori and pakeha girls. Pompallier largely failed in the task he was sent out to do; but he did succeed in laying the foundations of the Catholic church.

Hongi Hika, Te Rauparaha and Hone Heke — men of war

HONGI HIKA

The Europeans had given the Maori the musket. And the Maori, a skilled fighting race, made good use of it. Hongi Hika, a warrior of unusual powers, was born near Kaikohe, about

Maori canoe race

156

1770. He rapidly gained fame as a warrior and tactician and was soon to take advantage of the white man's god — *pu*, the gun.

By 1813 he owned several guns, bought from traders, and in 1814 he was further introduced to the white man's ways when Commander Dillon of the *Active* took Heke and some other Maoris for a trip to New South Wales. J. L. Nicholas described Hongi at this time:

> He had not the same robust figure as Ruatara, but his countenance was much more placid and seemed handsomer allowing for the operation of the tattoo, while it wanted the marked and animated severity which gave so decided a character to the face of his companion. The man had the reputation of being one of the greatest warriors in his country yet his natural disposition was mild and inoffensive, and he would appear to the attentive observer much more inclined to peaceful habits than to strife or enterprise.

By early 1817 Hongi had a following of about eight hundred fighting men and he and a lesser chief, Te Morenga, who had six hundred warriors and thirty-five muskets, planned several large wars of revenge. In January 1818 Te Morenga routed people living in the Tauranga area and in February Hongi attacked those in the area from Matetu to Hicks Bay. A year later when the war parties returned, Hongi off-loaded two thousand prisoners as well as canoe-loads of preserved heads.

Hongi's next spectacular move was a visit to England with Thomas Kendall and a fellow chief, Waikato, in August 1820. He spent five months in England, met King George IV and acquired an impressive array of gifts including a suit of chain armour. They finally left England in December, bound for Sydney where Hongi promptly exchanged all his gifts, except the suit of armour, for muskets, powder, lead, axes and swords. He reputedly arrived back in Auckland in July 1821 with three hundred muskets.

Two months later, under Hongi's command, an armada of fifty canoes, carrying about three thousand warriors, one thousand of them armed with muskets, left for the Auckland isthmus. The Ngapuhi army slaughtered the Ngatipaoa people and then continued to Thames to besiege the pa, Te Totara, stronghold of the Ngatimaru. Victorious, Hongi returned to the Bay of Islands in December 1822 with some two thousand prisoners. Two months later Hongi and his three thousand warriors attacked the Waikato tribes and about fifteen hundred of the unarmed tribesmen were killed by the northern army.

A year later they engaged in yet another battle; this time at the Bay of Plenty to avenge the death of some Ngapuhi warriors massacred at Green Lake, near Rotorua. The Te Arawa prepared for this battle by withdrawing to Mokoia Island in Lake Rotorua, but Hongi still managed to defeat them. His ultimate effort, the revenge on the Ngatiwhatua who had caused the death of many of his relatives, was in 1825. Hongi with five hundred men, all armed with muskets, defeated two thousand men armed with one musket. After this battle Hongi, aged almost fifty, rarely left the northern region. He was eventually wounded in a family dispute and died in March 1827. Augustus Earle paid him a visit in 1827 and described the meeting:

> In a beautiful bay surrounded by high rocks and overhanging trees, the chiefs sat in mute contemplation, their arms piled up in regular order on the beach. Hongi sat apart. Their richly ornamented war canoes were drawn up on the strand; some of the slaves were unloading stores; others were kindling fires. To me, it almost seemed to realise some of the passages of Homer, where he describes the wanderer Ulysses and his gallant band of warriors. We approached the chief and paid our respects to him. He received us kindly and with a dignified composure, as one accustomed to receiving homage. His look was emaciated, but so mild was the expression of his features that he would have been the last man I should have imagined accustomed to scenes of bloodshed and cruelty. But I soon remarked that when he became animated in conversation, his eyes sparkled with fire, and their expression changed, demonstrating that it only required his passions to be roused to exhibit him under a very different aspect....

Hongi Hika was one of the last great Maori warriors and exemplified a period of fierce Maori pride and dignity.

TE RAUPARAHA

Another great warrior, Te Rauparaha, was considered the most savage and unscrupulous of all Maoris. The settlers detested him, mainly because he kept destroying their plans to take possession of lands to which they had no clear title. Edward Wakefield in *Adventure in New Zealand*, describes Te Rauparaha as follows:

> His features are aquiline and striking: but an overhanging upper lip, and a retreating forehead, on which his eyebrows wrinkled back when he lifted his deep sunken eye-lids and penetrating eyes, produced a fatal effect on the good prestige arising from his first appearance. The great chieftain, the man able to lead others, and habituated to wield authority, was clear at first sight; but the savage ferocity of the tiger, who would not scruple to use any means for the attainment of that power, the destructive ambition of the selfish despot, was plainly discernible on a nearer view.

However, other, more favourable impressions have been given. The missionary, Richard Taylor, described him as a 'mild and gentlemanly Maori, if I may use the expression, though he was enveloped in a dirty blanket'. Te Rauparaha was a pre-European Maori and followed ancient codes. Central to his actions was the concept of *tika* which justified all actions that were in the interest of the tribe.

According to Maori standards he was a gentleman as his primary concern was for the security of his tribe. His reputation for ferocity was gained by his great military prowess. He won many victories often against numerically superior forces. Perhaps his most famous involvement with the Europeans was the incident of the Wairau massacre when a dispute of land rights culminated in the shooting of a party of armed Europeans. Te Rauparaha behaved with dignity throughout the incident and when Governor Fitzroy came down to Nelson to mediate, the Maoris were found to be in the right.

Governor Grey captured Te Rauparaha on a charge of treason in July 1846. He was held prisoner of war in Auckland for about eighteen months before being returned to Otaki where he died in 1849. Te Rauparaha was one of early New Zealand's most picturesque characters. He was a Maori of the old order, living and acting by old beliefs. As such he holds a place of honour in New Zealand's history.

Heke and his wife

HONE HEKE

Hone Heke, on the other hand, was most definitely a Maori of the new order, fighting not for the preservation of a traditional way of life, but for Maori equality in the new European society. He was a remote kinsman of Hongi Hika and his childhood was spent in the Bay of Islands. By 1831 he was on friendly terms with the missionaries Henry and William Williams, spending a lot of time at the Paihia mission station where he and his wife were baptised in 1835.

Heke supposedly supported the Treaty of Waitangi, being among the first to sway opinion towards acceptance of the Treaty and he was, despite the presence of greater chiefs, the first to sign the document. He was, however, not long in joining the doubters and was the first to take positive action to express the resentment growing amongst northern Maoris. In June 1840 he led a raiding party to the Waimate mission station, believing the missionaries to be in league with the Government to take over the country from the Maoris. From then until 1844 he was involved in minor skirmishes with the European whenever he felt some injustice had been done to the Maori people or some insult offered by the settlers.

On 8 July 1844 Heke cut down the flagstaff at Kororareka, demanding that two flags should be flown — the white man's and the Maori's. Overriding all his grievances was the belief that the Treaty was a trap, passing the *mana* of the land to the Queen and enslaving the Maori people. In January 1845 he again cut down the restored flagstaff and with an ally, chief Kawiti, led a successful attack on the township of Kororareka. Before Governor Fitzroy was ready to engage Heke and Kawiti, the friendly chief, Tamati Waka Nene, who had promised to defend the Governor and the British flag, opened hostilities against the rebel Maoris. Two wars were now in progress: Heke's war against the Europeans and a tribal war between Heke and Nene. On 12 June Heke was wounded and defeated in a battle with Nene. This virtually put him out of action and he showed little inclination to carry on the fighting. The final battle was on 11 January 1846, when Heke and Kawiti were conclusively defeated by the Europeans. They did not carry on resistance and were eventually granted a free pardon.

Tamati Waka Nene

Heke died four years later and after his death the tribes of the north erected a new flagstaff as a symbol of reconciliation. Heke had been torn between conflicting loyalties — he had no real wish to wage war on the Europeans and even protected mission property when war broke out. His sympathy with the European way of life probably made him more aware of the in-

sults and injuries done to his people by the white man. His dream was for the two races to live side by side in equality and harmony and he was the first Maori to think in terms not only of tribal honour but of Maori identity.

Edward Gibbon Wakefield — colonist

Edward Gibbon Wakefield was born in London on 20 March 1796, the son of a land agent and surveyor. His wayward youth culminated in three years imprisonment when in 1827 he kidnapped a wealthy young heiress and tricked her into marrying him. While languishing in Newgate prison he became interested in the art of colonisation and in 1829 produced an anonymous pamphlet: *Sketch of a Proposal for Colonising Australasia*, and later in the year, *A Letter from Sydney*.

Wakefield claimed to have discovered economic principles of 'systematic colonisation' which acted as clearly as mathematical laws. He argued that both the colonies and England suffered from an imbalance of land, labour and capital. Britain was overendowed with labour and capital and the threat of revolution was inherent in the grim living conditions of the unemployed poor. Wakefield believed that these conditions could be eased by exporting large numbers of the discontented to the colonies. In contrast to the situation in England, the colonies' development was being hindered by the easy acquisition of free or very cheap land. As a result labour was scarce and men of means were not interested in settling as they would have to become their own labourers. The population was widely scattered because of the ready availability of land and the people were living at subsistence level.

Wakefield's answer to these dilemmas was to sell colonial land at a fixed, uniform and high price so that the labourers did not become land owners until they had worked and saved for a few years. The uniformity of price would remove the possibility of cheaper land further out and foster concentrated, civilised settlements. His ideal colony was to be an agricultural settlement and the new colonial society would consist of a vertical section of English society, excluding the lowest level.

Theoretically it sounded fine; but in practice it was disastrous. Wakefield regarded New Zealand as a white man's country and in his colonial scheme ignored the presence of the Maori — a factor that was to cause much friction over the acquisition of land. He also failed to take into account such factors as the tendency of the capitalist system to undergo booms and slumps: the New Zealand Company's settlers were assailed by a severe slump in the early days of their settlement.

His ideas, however, were the genesis of colonisation in New Zealand. Following his tenets the New Zealand Company formed settlements at Port Nicholson (Wellington), New Plymouth and Nelson, and an auxiliary settlement grew up at Wanganui. His stimulation was also behind the religious settlements at Dunedin and Christchurch. With the foundation of the last two settlements, the Company's directors realised that its colonising activities were coming to an end. With the additional problem of financing difficulties, they terminated the Company's work in July 1850, selling their lands to the Government. After the Constitution Bill had been passed in 1852 Wakefield set sail for New Zealand to become involved in the country's politics. He was elected to both the House of Representatives and the Wellington Provincial Council in 1853. In 1855 he retired from the House of Representatives and a year later from the Provincial Council and died at his home in Wellington on 18 May 1862.

William Hobson — first Governor of New Zealand

Born at Waterford in Ireland in 1793, Hobson was the son of a local government lawyer. He joined the Navy at the age of ten and rose through the ranks reaching the rank of acting lieutenant at the age of twenty-three. In 1836 he was commanding the *Rattlesnake* which was sent to the Bay of Islands to protect British settlers and shipping threatened by the Maoris. When the British Government reluctantly conceded that it must become further involved in New Zealand's affairs and appoint a governor, Hobson was chosen.

He reached New Zealand in January 1840 armed with instructions to acquire sovereignty of the country and in February 1840 the Treaty of Waitangi was signed. The task that lay ahead of him was formidable: he had to both respect the rights of the Maori and at the same time guard the Crown's right of pre-emption of Maori lands. He was also hindered by the fact that he had to govern without military support and without any money to employ a strong Civil Service. The greatest obstacle he faced was lack of money. British economy was in a bad way and they chose not to divert funds from their two million poor to help the few thousand needy settlers in New Zealand. To maintain his civil and public works Hobson was drawing bills on his own Treasury and Britain was refusing to underwrite them. What little money that was made from land sales went to financing Hobson's government and administration rather than towards the stimulation of the settlement. The colony was under-capitalised and bound to stagnate through no fault of its new governor.

In September 1840 Hobson shifted the capital from Russell to Auckland, because of its more central position and this move created much tension with the New Zealand Company settlement at Port Nicholson who felt that their town should be the site for the capital. They further reviled Hobson because of his disapproval of their methods of land acquisition. *The New Zealand Gazette*, published in Port Nicholson, doubted that 'any Governor has ever had the disapprobation of a community so palpably expressed and so firmly maintained'.

Governing the new colony seemed to be an impossible task — apart from the financial problems Hobson was surrounded with other signs of failure: the settlers were scattered and defenceless and lived in constant fear of the Maoris. He did, however, do his best in a situation not conducive to success. Shortly after establishing his capital in Auckland he held his first legislative council meeting. Six ordinances concerning a judicial and administrative code were passed and another nineteen drafted. They covered matters ranging from a copyright for printed books, the control of harbours and the constitution of juries. Hobson was an innovator in building up a legal system which suited the environment of New Zealand rather than relying on the English judiciary system.

Beset by ill health Hobson died in 1842. At the time of his death a Maori chief wrote to Queen Victoria: 'Let not the new Governor be a boy or one puffed up; let not a troubler come amongst us; let him be a good man like this Governor who has just died.'

Sir George Grey — three times Governor

Born at Lisbon on 14 April 1812, George Grey entered the Royal Military College at Sandhurst in 1826. He then spent some time serving in London, a period which strengthened his ideals. 'I saw enough there,' he later wrote, 'to give a bias to my mind forever as to the necessity for change and reform. It was really from a desire to find relief from this misery that I went to Australia. . . . The effort to get lands, made by single individuals, seemed to me a wrong to humanity. To prevent such a monopoly in the new countries has been my task ever since.'

Sir George Grey

In 1838 Grey and Lieutenant Lushington, with the support of the Royal Geographical Society, set out on a voyage of discovery into the wilderness north of Perth in Australia. The voyage was not exceptionally successful. Unfriendly natives, ill health, floods and heavy rain plagued them. 'I could not but recall,' wrote Grey, 'that it had taken us ten days to reach a spot by which the proper route was only a short day's journey from the valley we were first camped in, and that in our march through the country . . . we had lost seven ponies and

injured many of those remaining.' After convalescing from a wound in his hip Grey took the post of Resident Magistrate at Albany. His reports on the Aborigines and ideas on the 'colonisation of natives' impressed the Colonial Office and in 1840 he was appointed Governor of the new colony of South Australia.

In 1845 he was appointed to the post of Lieutenant-Governor of New Zealand. At this time, the editor of the *South Australian* pointed out that Grey was to take over New Zealand 'in the most miserable, ruinous and almost irretrievable condition'. Adding, 'We do not doubt his complete success, for nothing is impossible to men like him.' And so Grey began his first New Zealand governorship which lasted from 1845 to 1853. He had the aid of a generous parliamentary grant and the help from naval and military factions — support that he badly needed as he arrived in the middle of the wars in the north.

His first act was to settle Hone Heke's insurrection. He marched against this chief and his allies with a force of twelve hundred soldiers and by 1846 he had succeeded in quelling these rebellious Maoris. He then moved his army down to Wellington and drove the insurgents into the mountains, capturing Te Rauparaha in the process. His next attack was on the missionaries whom he respected but who, he was adamant, should have no political influence. He used two bullets to get rid of the powerful Henry Williams: he first charged him with inciting the northern Maoris to revolt and then he despatched a recommendation to Gladstone that 'individuals cannot be put in possession of these tracts of land [that the missionaries had bought] without a large expenditure of British blood and money'. Williams was dismissed.

Grey's ambition was to provide New Zealand with a democratic form of government. He abolished high property qualifications thus giving many of the poorer classes the right to vote. But he took his time in allowing representative government.

He felt that self-government would precipitate a general Maori war as the colonists were still a minority and not yet to be trusted with the powers of government. Instead he divided New Zealand into two provinces; New Ulster and New Munster, and it was not until 1852 that Grey thought the time was ripe to institute representative government.

In 1853 Grey departed for the governorship at Cape Town. He returned to New Zealand for a second term of office from 1861 to 1868 and in 1874 became a member of the House of Representatives, serving as Prime Minister from 1877 to 1879. Vogel, who had preceded Grey, had introduced a boom period in New Zealand life by large injections of borrowed funds. This large scale borrowing continued, £3.5 million being borrowed in 1878 and £5 million in 1879. Land prices also reached their height during this period. But the portents for disaster were evident and when the Grey government went out of office in October 1879 New Zealand headed for an economic depression that was worldwide.

In ill health, Grey remained on the Opposition benches for another eleven years and left Wellington for England in 1894. He died in England in September 1898. As a politician he was not really successful. A contemporary said of him: 'He quarrelled with enemies and he quarrelled with friends. The only people he did not quarrel with were the public and the Maoris, both of whom he treated like children.' He did have a real understanding of the Maori mind but his achievements — which were notable — were limited by an arrogance and an unwillingness to accept orders. One of the most lasting things that Grey left New Zealand was his mansion and the exotic introduced animal and plant life on Kawau Island.

James McKenzie — legendary stock rustler

One of the more infamous characters of New Zealand's early days was McKenzie, a sheep stealer, whose very name today conjures up romance and bravado. Few facts are known about him and what knowledge does exist is probably suspect, romanticised by the early pioneers. The only documented facts about his early life are contained in a petition that he made for his release from jail in 1855.

Here McKenzie states that he was a native of Inverness-shire and that his father was 'an Officer of high rank in the British Service, but unfortunately he died in the Island of Ceylon when Your Petitioner was a child, leaving his family in needy circumstances'. In the late 1840s he emigrated to Melbourne, Australia, and later moved on to New Zealand where he worked his way overland from Nelson to Otago. The petition goes on to say that, while waiting for boundaries to be surveyed on a thousand-acre property that he had applied for, he drove some sheep from Canterbury to Otago for a man called James Mossman and this led to a charge of sheep stealing.

That was McKenzie's account. A more satisfactory account of McKenzie's activities was written by Herries Beattie who built up his chronology from a number of sources in the area. According to Beattie, McKenzie was born in the highlands in 1820, spent some time in Australia, arrived in Nelson in 1850 and explored the South Island from then until 1852. In 1853 he stole five hundred sheep from the 'Levels' station in South Canterbury, drove them to Southland and hid them. He then stole more sheep from the South Canterbury area and left these in the Omarama district. After visiting several stations on the Mataura and Clutha rivers and north Otago he stole a further thousand sheep from the 'Levels'. On 15 March 1855 he was caught and sentenced to five years' hard labour. After two escape bids he was pardoned in January 1856 and released. Early in 1857 he left New Zealand for good.

Those are the bare bones. The legends that developed about him and his activities are another story. A Lytttelton sheriff described him: 'Height about five foot eleven inches; light coloured hair; small grey eyes; large aquiline nose; long thin face; spare muscular body. He speaks English imperfectly and feigns generally that he understands only gaelic. He has a peculiar habit of putting his hands behind him and snapping his fingers.' He was a loner, intense in appearance, a strange and enigmatic man. If he was guilty as charged he would have been an exceptional shepherd to move hundreds of sheep at a time down across the MacKenzie Country rivers, over mountain passes to Central Otago, across the mighty Clutha River and over more mountains and rivers in Southland — distances of up to six hundred kilometres.

Whether McKenzie was innocent and failed to defend himself because of his lack of understanding of the English language or whether he was the amazing sheep-rustler that legend makes him out to be are still debatable questions. Whatever he was, McKenzie and his super-dog 'Friday' with their legendary exploits have become a myth in New Zealand folk history.

Wiremu Tamihana — father of the King Movement

Born near Hamilton in about 1802, Wiremu Tamihana was the son of a famous war leader, Te Waharoa, chief of the Ngatihaua tribe. After his father's death he took the name Te Waharoa and the chieftaincy. As a young man he accompanied his father on war expeditions but when he was baptised in 1839, taking on the name William Thompson (Wiremu Tamihana), he refused to take part in further wars. He was a man of great intelligence and Christian convictions. Wrote Sir John Gorst in the *Maori King*: 'he argues on religious maxims and intersperses his writings with Biblical quotations, in what appears to us an unusual degree. It would be a mistake to suppose this the result of cant or hypocrisy.' Tamihana further proved his peaceful intentions by, with the help of other converted Maoris, building a separate pa at a distance from the main tribal pa.

Wiremu Tamihana

His wisdom extended to political matters. British annexation had brought problems to the Maori race and lawlessness was a growing problem. In 1856 Wiremu Tamihana approached the Native Office in Auckland to suggest that Maori laws should be drawn up and enforced by Maori magistrates. His suggestions were ignored and on his return from Auckland he visited the Waikato chief, Potatau Te Wherowhero, asking him to help him organise meetings to make their own law and elect their own King.

He was thus the founder of the King Movement and played a leading role in calling the meetings that culminated in June 1858 in Potatau being accepted by many Maoris as their King. 'If all the Kings of the different islands were from Rome alone,' wrote Tamihana, 'from thence also might come one for here; but is not the Queen a native of England, Nicholas of Russia, Bonaparte of France and Pomara of Tahiti — each from his own people? ... each nation is separate, and I also ... must have a King for myself.'

At the election of Potatau, Wiremu Tamihana told the people that the new King would 'be a covering for the lands of New Zealand which still remain in our possession'. The King would also 'restrain the father who is badly disposed towards his son, and the elder brother who would take advantage of the younger brother. He will manifest his displeasure in regard to that which is evil; he will do away with the works of confusion and disorder.' His idea was to establish a united nation of Maori tribes with their own national leader who would protect them from the iniquities of the white man and maintain law and order within the Maori race.

War broke out in the Taranaki in 1860 and some of the Maori King's supporters went off to fight with Wiremu Kingi. Tamihana, although he thought Kingi had been treated unjustly, was against fighting the pakeha. Early in 1861 he set off for Taranaki to see if he could make peace. A truce was negotiated and Kingi declared that he placed the dispute in Tamihana's hands to settle. The British invited him to Auckland to discuss the matter with the Governor, but Tamihana, fearing he would be kidnapped by Grey as Te Rauparaha had been, declined and fighting broke out again. Tamihana returned to the Waikato, disappointed but still believing in and desiring peace.

When Grey instigated the war in the Waikato, Tamihana was a reluctant participant often wanting to surrender but being persuaded to fight on by his men. In 1865 General Casey and Wiremu Tamihana finally made peace. Much of his land was confiscated by the Government and when Tamihana went to Wellington to ask for the return of his lands, he was refused. He returned to the Waikato where he died a year later. Wiremu Tamihana was one of the most outstanding Maoris of early New Zealand. Sir John Gorst wrote of him: 'I have met many statesmen in the course of my long life, but none superior in intellect and character to this Maori chief, whom most people would look upon as a savage.'

Sir William Fox — Prohibitionist and Premier

William Fox was born on 9 June 1812 in Durham, England. After obtaining a Bachelor of Arts and Master of Arts he was called to the Bar in 1842 but left a few months later for New Zealand where he became editor of the *New Zealand Gazette* and *Britannia Spectator*. In 1843, after the death of Captain Arthur Wakefield in the Wairau Massacre, Fox took over his position as resident agent for the New Zealand Company at Nelson and after the death of Colonel William Wakefield he succeeded him as Principal Agent for the New Zealand Company.

Fox first entered politics on the provincial level, serving on the Wellington Provincial Council and in the 1855 general election he was elected to the General Assembly as a member for Wanganui. For the next thirty years, William Fox was to be a household name in New Zealand politics — serving as Premier four times. His first term of office was in 1856 when he and other Provincialists defeated Sewell, taking his place for only a few weeks. When he again became Premier in 1861 he gained a reputation for hypocrisy towards the Maoris: he argued that Stafford's ministry had embarked upon a disastrous campaign against the Maoris and the campaign had been terminated by a 'disgraceful peace' with the Maoris being unfairly treated. But later in office he strongly supported the Maori Wars arguing that the natives would benefit from them as '... nothing has been or can be more pernicious to the native race, than the possession of large territories under tribal title'.

At the end of 1869 Fox returned for his third term in office, passing a curious legislation known as the Disturbed Districts Act which allowed for such things as deportation, the binding of convicts to service at sea and imprisonment without trial. This term in office, along with his final term for a few weeks in 1873, did not show Fox as a policymaker. He was becoming the tool of more astute men who pulled the strings while he took centre stage. After his fourth stint as Premier Fox did not hold ministerial office again. He was involved in a different cause: that of temperance. In 1886 he founded the New Zealand Alliance, believing that 'The drinking habits of the day are ruining the national character.'

In 1878 he again took his seat in the House and his last official role was as Land Claims Commissioner in the early 1880s. Still energetic at the age of eighty he climbed Mt Egmont. In 1893 he died.

Fox was a man who despite his long involvement in New Zealand politics never really made an impact on the country's history. Octavius Hadfield wrote of him; 'He seems to make strangers think a great deal of him. He really can do nothing but talk. He is very shallow and ignorant — very illogical. I do not think he can see the connection between premises and conclusion. He cannot enter at all into the spirit of the British Constitution.' However, if Fox did not manage to bequeath any startling political reforms to New Zealand he did leave another type of heritage. He was a gifted landscape artist and several of his paintings remain in New Zealand today.

Te Ua and Te Kooti — spiritual warriors

TE UA

The final phases of the Maori wars were dominated by two men and their religions. Several Maori religious movements had been in existence since the 1830s, most of them trying to express parts of the Bible in ways that would be pertinent to the Maori way of life, often in ways that horrified the more traditional European Christian. Pai Marire, the 'good and peaceful' movement was one such cult and its leader was Te Ua.

Te Ua, 'the Prophet', whose real name was

Horopapera Tuwhakararo, first learned of Christianity when he was a prisoner of war in the Hokianga area. When he was released he became a teacher in Taranaki and was baptised. He was supposedly visited by the Archangel Gabriel who advised changes in religious customs. Two events reputedly occurred which gained followers for Te Ua's cult: he broke apart ropes and chains that bound him after an alleged assault on a Maori woman, and he was commanded to kill his son whose wounds were then miraculously healed by the Angel Gabriel.

The Maori Wars were the main factor that swelled Te Ua's congregation — his teachings gave them hope at a time when nearly all hope was lost. He declared the Christian religion false and proclaimed that if the Maori people were to follow him New Zealand would be rid of the Europeans and once the white men were gone men would be sent from heaven to teach all the European arts and sciences. Central to the religion was the belief that the converts were possessed of a power that would make them impervious to bullets if, when under fire, they raised their right hand and cried 'Pai marire, hau! Hau!'

Te Ua's followers thus became known as the Hau hau and they demonstrated incredible boldness in battle. The first Hau hau attacks were made at Te Ahuahu in Taranaki and after a small victory, on the Angel Gabriel's instructions, Te Ua exhumed and dried the head of Captain Lloyd who had been killed in battle. The head was henceforth to be the means of Jehovah's communication with his Maori people.

By the end of 1864 the movement was rapidly gaining in strength. The Maori King, Potatau II, allied himself with the movement. In time all Maoris opposing the Government were known as Hau haus irrespective of their religious beliefs. After a series of particularly savage battles Te Ua was captured in 1866. He renounced his beliefs and much of his following and teachings died away.

Pai Marire was a curious mixture of Old Testament morality, Christian doctrine and primitive Maori beliefs. Te Ua proclaimed that New Zealand was Canaan, the Maoris, Jews, and the Book of Moses, their laws. Many of his chants and incantations were based on Christian prayers. On the other hand cannabalism was revived and men and women were exhorted to live together promiscuously to compensate for the depopulation caused by battle and European disease.

The movement gained such an overwhelming popularity amongst the Maoris because it gave a spiritual belief to the success of their cause at a time when the cause was objectively hopeless. The teachings led the Maoris to believe that they were a second Chosen People and with divine aid they would return from the wilderness to their hereditary lands. Pai Marire drove the people to fanatical and violent behaviour but it was an important development in Maori religious history forming a bridge between early Maori attempts to express Christianity in terms relevant to their own social structure and formally instituted churches. It heralded the emergence of more formal Maori churches.

It was inevitable that the movement should die when the circumstances in which it arose — battle and bloodshed — ceased, and the needs to which it responded ceased to exist. But vestiges of the cult did rise again later in a different form as the Ringatu faith devised by Te Kooti who was renowned as the last leader of an armed opposition against the European.

TE KOOTI

There is little known about Te Kooti's early life. He was born at Matawhero near Gisborne but the date of his birth is unknown. Documentation of his life begins in 1865 when he was exiled to the Chatham Islands, almost certainly unjustly, on suspicion of being in league with the Hau haus. On the Chathams Te Kooti won for himself a position of leadership. He developed a flair for prophetic sayings, won his fellow prisoners over to his new creed and led them in daily prayer.

The creed he developed was based on the scriptures from which he discovered a special significance for the number twelve and the twelfth day of each month was to be set aside for worship. He also borrowed a sign from the Hau hau creed that was to become the name of his sect: the Upraised Hand — Ringatu.

In 1868 his promises to the prisoners of deliverance from captivity turned into reality in the form of the arrival of the schooner the *Rifleman*. He freed his fellow prisoners, captured the boat and a few days later landed at Whareongaonga on the mainland.

Te Kooti

He and his followers then proceeded to move inland, hotly pursued by search parties. On 8 August, about a month after he landed, a search party caught up with him and an inconclusive battle was fought. Enraged by this and his unjust imprisonment, Te Kooti, who had up till now shown peaceable intentions, took the initiative and attacked Poverty Bay. He was a master of guerilla warfare and in the bush being practically undefeatable, achieved spectacular successes. His two greatest defeats were in fortified positions: on a ridge at Makaretu and an old pa at Ngatapa.

In March and April 1869 he made raids on the Bay of Plenty and on Mohaka in Hawke's Bay. The settlers were becoming terrified by his swift movement from one coast to another and the Government decided on a policy to starve him out of the mountains, destroying fences around potato crops and letting the wild pigs take their toll. The ruse was successful and in June 1869 Te Kooti came out of the mountains heading for Taupo in search of provisions. Troops had moved into the area but Te Kooti was too quick for them. He evaded his captors and built a small pa at Te Porere, near the headwaters of the Wanganui River. Soldiers attacked him here in October 1869, but Te Kooti and about two hundred and fifty followers escaped.

Te Kooti, probably tired of all the skirmishing, then made a bid for peace but his offer was rejected. Further enraged, he launched an all-out attack on the Arawa tribe, the most resolute

tribe supporting the Government. This failed and for the next two years he travelled throughout the Urewera, pursued by Maori contingents under European officers. By May 1872 he had had enough and escaped to the sanctuary of the King Country. In 1883 he was granted an official pardon and was given land in the Bay of Plenty on which he built a church.

He preached a fundamentalist type of religion — the strict truth of the Holy Writ was taught but he interpreted the truth in his own way, giving mystical significance to passages which caught his imagination. His teachings were in the Maori tongue and applied to Maori situations. This did much to bridge that same gap that Pai Marire did — the gap between Christian teachings of the missionaries and the adaptation of these teachings to the Maori way of life.

Te Kooti was a paradoxical man: he was a fierce warrior and known to the Europeans as the 'arch fiend' but he was also a man of devout religious beliefs. Perhaps if justice had been done in 1865 and he had not been accused of treachery he would have remained a man of peace. He died from injuries he received in 1893 when run over by a cart. His followers erected a monument to him and the words on it describe him best: both a prophet and a warrior.

Sir Julius Vogel — politician of renown

Of all the early politicians it was Vogel who had the most extraordinary impact on New Zealand. Born in London in 1835, Vogel was brought up by his grandfather and at the age of sixteen decided to seek his fortune in Australia. In preparation for this he took a course in metallurgy and then sailed for Australia in 1852. With a friend he set up a company of assayers and retailers in Victoria; but not with much success.

After a period of wandering around the goldfields Vogel then became editor of the *Maryborough and Dunolly Advertiser* in 1857. Conditions on the goldfields were becoming depressed and business was slow so in 1861 Vogel moved to the newly opened goldfields in Otago. Here he joined the *Otago Witness* and later in the year, with the aid of the editor of the *Witness*, founded New Zealand's first daily newspaper, the *Otago Daily Times*.

Vogel had had an early interest in politics; in fact, in Australia he had unsuccessfully contested a seat in the Victoria Legislative Council. He carried this interest with him to New Zealand and after twice contesting seats for the House of Representatives he was elected to the Otago Provincial Council in 1863 and at the end of 1866 he became the Provincial Treasurer and the strongest man on the Council.

His main platforms at this time were provincial rights and the strengthening of the bonds between England and New Zealand. When William Fox was asked to form a government in 1869 he asked Vogel to become Colonial Treasurer. And so began Vogel's greatest years. New Zealand was in the middle of a slump with a stagnant economy. The stage was set for some innovative political management. Vogel believed that with improved communications to open up the country further and the resulting increase of immigration a new vitality would be injected into the economy. He proposed that over the next ten years, £10 million should be spent on roads, railways and people. The money would be found from land sales, railway profits and the remainder borrowed on the security of land set aside as a public estate.

The next decade saw exciting progress: over one hundred thousand assisted immigrants arrived in the country, communications advanced rapidly and almost £20 million was borrowed by the Government.

However, trouble arose. The provincial governments were hindering the progress of Vogel's scheme by refusing to set aside securities and demanding expensive, often unnecessary public works. In 1874 Vogel, the former staunch provincialist, put a resolution through Parliament that abolished the provincial form of government in the North Island. His successor, Harry Atkinson, later expanded Vogel's resolution and the South Island provincial governments were also abandoned.

Vogel had gained an enormous following from the prosperity engendered by his immigration and public works policy. In April 1873 he became Premier. But in the final years of the decade, depression once again loomed, and Vogel just as quickly became extremely unpopular and was blamed for the high level of unemployment and the vast outstanding loans. These judgements were, however, unduly harsh. He was not responsible for the heavy borrowing, stressing throughout that expenditure must be kept in check and at the same time advising that the level of immigration should not be too high. It was a situation where his basically sound policies had been over-extended and the blame lay with the political and economic structure of the period, not with Vogel.

Vogel's policy of development is what he is best remembered for but he did many other things at this time to contribute to New Zealand's development. He helped found the Government Life Insurance Department in 1869 and the Public Trust Office in 1872, and he was forever advocating imperial expansion into the Pacific and trade links with Australia and the United States. He travelled to Australia three times to discuss intercolonial interest and the United Kingdom twice to negotiate loans.

On a trip to England in 1874 he fell ill and had to resign from the office of Premier. Returning to New Zealand in 1876 he resumed office for six months when he announced his retirement from New Zealand politics, intending to return to the United Kingdom to improve his personal financial position. His separation from New Zealand was not to be complete; he was appointed Agent General, a position which required him to look after New Zealand's political and business interests in the United Kingdom, and in 1878 he joined the board of the New Zealand Agricultural Company, a speculative London company formed to buy and settle land in the South Island. This latter move led to him being asked to resign from the Agent Generalship because it was felt that a man holding such a position should not be involved in private business ventures in New Zealand.

By 1884 the New Zealand Agricultural Company was on the brink of collapse and Vogel returned to New Zealand to try and consolidate its position. Believing that the success of the company depended on Government intervention, he once again entered politics and successfully contested the seat of Christchurch North. A new Government was formed by Vogel and Robert Stout but it could not solve the country's economic problems and was voted out in 1887. Vogel kept his seat but in 1888 left to visit England; he stayed there and in 1889 resigned from Parliament. He died in London on 12 March 1899.

Vogel's greatest achievement was development of the era of expansion — the early 1870s when his forward-thinking economic policies, enthusiasm and stimulation brought new hope and life to a society that was stagnating both economically and politically. Despite the fact that he was made a scapegoat for the depressed years of the late 1870s, he was a politician who aroused much admiration and retains a special place in New Zealand's history.

Richard Seddon — King Dick

The most loved of all New Zealand's early politicians was Richard John Seddon, the champion of the underdog. He was born in Lancashire, England, in 1845 and although the son of two teachers left school at the age of twelve and after doing some farm work and working as an apprentice in an ironworks he migrated to Australia at the age of eighteen. After failing to strike it rich in the Australian goldfields in 1866 he was tempted by the promise of golden riches in New Zealand and left for the West Coast where he became a storekeeper and hotelier.

He soon became interested in politics and in 1879 entered Parliament. The Liberal Party had its beginnings in the 1880s and to Seddon it was just what the country needed. Seddon was violently opposed to the power the wealthy families wielded over the populace. 'It is the rich and the poor; it is the wealthy people and the landowners against the middle classes and the labouring classes' was his view of the presiding political order. An expert at Parliamentary tactics and a fluent speaker, Seddon soon became a notable member of the Liberal Party and became Minister of Public Works when the Liberal Party, under John Ballance, came to power in 1891. When Ballance died in 1893 Richard Seddon became Premier.

Many reforms took place under his Premiership, probably the most famous being the introduction of Old Age Pensions in 1898. There was much poverty in New Zealand in the 1880s and 1890s and the old people suffered in particular. Many people believed that the State had no responsibility for their plight but Seddon insisted it did and a seven shilling a week pension was instigated. Other reforms introduced by Seddon involved legislation to provide for maternity hospitals and infant care, and the introduction of a system of free places in secondary schools — a step towards his dream of free education to university level. He established a State Fire Insurance Office in 1903 and in the same year increased the Old Age Pension to ten shillings a week.

He was also, like Vogel, renowned for his imperialism, being devoted to the British Empire. He had dreams of a Pacific Empire being ruled by New Zealand and was furious when Britain allowed other nations to enter the Pacific, stoutly maintaining that Britain should annex these territories for herself.

Seddon was achieving much for New Zealand and in 1905 was again returned to power, saying, 'so long as I can hold on to the control of affairs in New Zealand I shall do so'. He was still in power when he died in 1906.

His rule was a long one and a popular one; the people he legislated for, the mother and the infant, the young, the worker, and the elderly — nearly the whole population — all loved him and all voted for him. He was a people's man, his recipe for electoral success being summed up by him as follows: 'Enjoin upon him [i.e. the candidate] the necessity of a house to house canvass, nothing goes down so well with the sturdy tillers of the soil as a personal chat.... Ten minutes talk on irrigation and a little judicious flattery as to breed of stock, crops etc. and to wind up with the cost of carrying grain as compared with that of timber and minerals etc., on your railways with a promise to have a searching enquiry made into the same, would fetch the vote.'

He was also a man of the people; he was not opposed to a drink or two, exuded genial good fellowship and, as he himself admitted, never knew where to put his aitches. His personal charisma, the disarray of the Parliamentary Opposition and the fact that New Zealand was ready and receptive to the Liberal humanitarian type of government ensured that 'King Dick's' reign was to be long and successful.

Green and white at Winchester — the predominant colours of the New Zealand pastoral scene. (Kendall)

The long harbour of the Gallic-flavoured colony of Akaroa provides the perfect setting for fishing boats and pleasure craft. (Prenzel)

Fishermen prepare for the whitebait run on one of the many rivers near Waikouaiti. (Kendall)

Overleaf: *Banks Peninsula was originally named Banks Island by Cook when he first mapped New Zealand. The error was detected in 1809 when Captain Chase attempted to sail his ship Pegasus between 'island' and shore. (Prenzel)*

Opposite, above:
The 'Edinburgh of the South' — Dunedin — seen from Signal Hill. (Fairlie)

Opposite, below:
The University of Otago, Dunedin — New Zealand's first university. The complex retains its 1878 slate-roofed, bluestone buildings. (Fairlie)

Dunedin has a unique charm, with architecture from the last century such as this private residence. (Kendall)

Gateway to Otago — the peaceful 21-kilometre-long harbour. (Kendall)

Opposite: *Picturesque Lake Waihola, south of Dunedin. (Waite)*

Overleaf: *Lake Wanaka. According to Maori legend, Chief Te Rakaihautu dug out the lake and the mountain ranges were formed by the discarded earth. (Kendall)*

Muted hues of lupins bring colour to the roadside near Balclutha. (Robinson)

The motorbike replaces the horse for this shepherd in Central Otago. (Kendall)

Right: *Golden highlights at Albert Town, near Lake Wanaka. (Kendall)*

Below: *Once the height of luxury to miners in the area, the Cardrona Hotel in the Crown Range still presents its wavy facade to the thirsty traveller. (Collinson)*

Opposite, above and below: *The gold rush gave birth to Arrowtown whose mining cottages and century-old sycamores are a great tourist attraction. (Collinson, Waite)*

Overleaf: *The gold rush days are over but the giant deciduous trees of Central Otago light up the countryside with a different type of gold during the autumn months. (Kendall)*

Opposite: *Snowy peaks brood over a high-country sheep station near Queenstown. (Collinson)*

Bottom: *Shearer's cottage, Queenstown. (Collinson)*

Below and overleaf: *Queenstown — town of lakes, mountains and hotels — steeped in the history of gold mining days. (Collinson, Kendall, Prenzel)*

A deer on the hillside at Kelvin Heights, near Queenstown. (Prenzel)

Left: *The fisherman casts his line into the tranquillity of Lake Wakatipu. The Z-shaped lake has a depth extending to well below sea level. (Prenzel)*

Below: *Early morning greets the Remarkables — one of the most celebrated sights of Central Otago. (Collinson)*

Bottom: *Lake Hayes, called Wai-Whakaata by the Maoris — 'water that reflects light'. (Kendall)*

Opposite, above: *An oasis among mountains, Lake Kilpatrick near Queenstown. (Kendall)*

Opposite, below: *The outlet of Lake Wakatipu, third largest lake in New Zealand. (Collinson)*

Above: *The Kawarau River, draining out of Lake Wakatipu, is a violent, tempestuous stretch of water. Its name is Maori for 'many rapids'. (Prenzel)*

The many coloured hues of the Frankston Flats, near Queenstown. (Kleinpaste)

Jetboating on the Shotover River. (Watson)

Opposite: *Coronet Peak — a popular ski field operating since 1948. (Collinson)*

Trademark of Milford Sound, Fiordland — the sharp outline of Mitre Peak (1412 metres). (Prenzel)

The Shotover, flanked by the snowy ranges of Coronet Peak. (Collinson)

Right: *Bowen Falls, named after an early Governor of New Zealand, cascade from a high valley in Milford. (Collinson)*

Opposite, above left: *The high vertical walls flanking Doubtful Sound rise sheer from the sea. Cook named the Sound 'Doubtfull Harbour' in 1770. (Fairlie)*

Opposite, above right: *The Kepler Mountains dominate the horizon at Manapouri in Fiordland. (Fairlie)*

Opposite, below: *Mt Balloon rises to 1829 metres to the east of the MacKinnon Pass. (Fairlie)*

Lake Te Anau, largest lake in the South Island, sprawls at the feet of high rugged mountains. (Prenzel)

MacKinnon Pass on the Milford Track — one of the finest walks in the world. (Fairlie)

Opposite: Fiordland, one of the wettest places on earth and the wildest and most isolated part of New Zealand. (Kleinpaste)

The Jervois Glacier on Mt Elliott on the Milford Track. (Fairlie)

Top: *The unhurried pace of life on Stewart Island. (Fairlie)*

Above: *The unspoilt stretch of Tautuku Beach on the south-east coast of the South Island. (Fairlie)*

Left: *The Hollyford River, Fiordland. (Kleinpaste)*

Above: *View across Stewart Island from Observation Rock. (Fairlie)*

Below: *Golden Bay, Stewart Island. (Fairlie)*

5

Places of interest in
New Zealand

The following is a very brief indication of places of interest in New Zealand. Far more detailed information can be obtained from local tourist centres or from the Automobile Association of New Zealand.

NORTHLAND

Whangarei
Clapham Clock Collection, Vine St
Mair Park, at the foot of Mt Parahaki
Society of Arts Gallery, Quay St
Whangarei Falls, on the road to Ngunguru
Environs
Marsden oil-fired power station, south of the city
Glorat museum, 5 km west
Tutukaka, deep sea fishing, 29 km north
Sandy Bay and Woolley Bay, 40 km
Wairau Falls, on the road to Kaikohe
Kamo, mineral springs, 7 km north

Bay of Islands
One of New Zealand's most popular holiday areas and top big game fishing centre. The Cream Trip is one of the finest launch trips in the country. (*See* Russell, Waitangi and Kerikeri).

Dargaville
Dargaville Museum contains items of local historical interest. Good toheroa can be found in season at Bayly's Beach.

Houhora Heads
Extensive displays of Maori artefacts, kauri gum, whaling and Victoriana at the Wagener Museum.

Kaikohe
The Hone Heke Monument is of interest. The town is one of the largest Maori centres in New Zealand.

Kaitaia
Principal town of the far north with bus trips leaving from here to Cape Reinga and Ninety Mile beach. Far North Regional Museum has interesting displays of the district's history.

Kerikeri
Picturesque citrus growing and craft centre. Of interest are the Kerikeri Mission House, the Stone Store, craft centre and museum at Hui Te Rangiora, Rewa's Village, the Kororipo Pa, Rainbow Falls, Peacock Gardens, the Kaeo-Kerikeri Union Parish Church, the Red Barn and Black Sheep (crafts). Inland is the Puketi Forest which includes an impressive stand of young kauris.

Ninety Mile Beach
A stretch of white sand beach from west of Kaitaia to near Cape Maria van Diemen. Good surf fishing and toheroa season in winter.

Ngawha Springs
Hot mercury and sulphur springs situated between Ohaewai and Kaikohe. A historical museum and courthouse are nearby at Puketona.

Opononi
Site of the annual Axeman's Carnival in January and past home of 'Opo', a friendly wild dolphin who made the town famous in the 1950s.

Puhoi

First settled by German-speaking Bohemians. Places of interest include the Puhoi Hotel, Wayside Calvary and Church of St Peter and St Paul.

Rawene

An old timber town with items of interest such as an 1877 Maori fishing canoe and Clendon House, residence of the first United States Consul in New Zealand.

Russell

The first centre of European settlement in New Zealand. Places of interest include Christ Church, Pompallier House, Flagstaff Hill, the Centennial Russell Museum. Nearby are Moturua Island (Marion du Fresne's shore base), Opua and beach resort at Paihia.

Waimate North

The Waimate Mission House is the second oldest building in New Zealand. The town was the site of the first Christian European marriage in the country and New Zealand's oldest oak tree grows here.

Waipoua Forest Sanctuary

Contains the largest remaining kauri forest in New Zealand. Points of interest in the forest include *Tanemahuta* (a massive kauri) and Maxwell Cottage which houses a display of the life and tools of a kauri bushman. Just south of the forest sanctuary is Trounson Kauri Park, noted for the Four Sisters, a kauri tree with four trunks.

Waipu

A farming centre originally settled by Scottish Highlanders. Waipu Cove and Langs Beach are both popular for swimming, surfing and fishing and the Waipu House of Memories contains relics of the town's early settlement.

Waitangi

Site of the signing of the Treaty of Waitangi. Places of interest include the Treaty House, the kauri flagstaff and the Maori Centennial Memorial Meeting House. Nearby are Mt Bledisloe (magnificent views of the Bay of Islands), the Haruru Falls on the Waitangi River and the Museum of Shipwrecks aboard the *Tui* at Waitangi Bridge.

Warkworth

A satellite earth station is situated a few kilometres south of here. Oyster farms can be found on the Mahurangi River. In the town: Parry Kauri Park and Kowhai Park.

Whangaroa

Popular base for big game fishing. The beautiful, nearly land-locked, harbour can be seen by launch trips operating out of the town. Nearby at Kaeo is New Zealand's first Methodist Mission, 'Wesleydale'.

AUCKLAND AND ENVIRONS

Hauraki Gulf

Stretching from the Poor Knight Islands in the north to the Firth of Thames, this area contains numerous islands and is a haven for yachtsmen and deep sea fishermen. Most popular islands include the Poor Knights, excellent for diving; Kawau, featuring Sir George Grey's former Mansion House; Great Barrier and Little Barrier; Waiheke; Rangitoto and Pakatoa, developed as a holiday resort.

North of Auckland

Helensville, 50 km north of Auckland. Noted for the Parakai Hot Springs, Pioneer Museum and historic courthouse

Orewa, popular seaside resort, 40 km north of Waiwera. Orewa Marineland is of interest

Waiwera, 48 km north of Auckland, seaside resort popular for hot thermal springs

Wenderholm Reserve, beach and riverside picnic park just north of Waiwera

Whangaparoa Peninsula, about 37 km north of Auckland, offers many beaches and sheltered coves

Auckland City and Environs

Auckland City Art Gallery, Wellesley St East

Auckland Town Hall, cnr Greys Ave and Queen St

The Supreme Courthouse, Waterloo Quadrant

Public Library, Lorne St

Synagogue, Greys Ave

Cathedral of Holy Trinity, Parnell

202

Parnell Rose Gardens, Gladstone Rd
Ewelme Cottage, Ayr St
The Savage Memorial and Gardens, Bastion Pt
Selwyn Domain, Mission Bay
Viewpoints: One Tree Hill, Mt Eden, Mt Albert
Auckland Domain, entrances off Stanley St and Park Rd
Cornwall Park, Greenlane West Rd
Albert Park, central city
Zoological Gardens, off Great North Rd
Ellerslie Race Course, Greenlane East
Museum of Transport and Technology, Great North Rd
Melanesian Mission Museum, Tamaki Drive
Fernglen Native Plant Museum, Birkenhead
Auckland Museum, Auckland Domain
Botanic Garden, Manurewa
Totara Park, Manurewa
Domain Winter Gardens, Auckland Domain
Waitakere Ranges, West Auckland
Parnell Village shopping complex, Parnell
St Stephen's Chapel, Parnell
Selwyn Court, Parnell
Alberton, Mt Albert Rd
Auckland Observatory, One Tree Hill Domain
Fine beaches on North Shore and West Coast

SOUTH AUCKLAND AND WAIKATO

Hamilton

Hamilton Lake Domain, Ruakiwi Rd
Waikato Art Gallery and Museum, London St
Waikato University, Hillcrest Rd
Hamilton Gardens, Cobham Drive
Ferrybank Park, Grantham St
Rangiriri gun boat, Memorial Drive
Founders' Memorial Theatre, London and Tristram Sts

Environs
Templeview Mormon Temple, 7 km south-west
Hilldale Game Farm, 8 km off the road to Whatawhata
Te Rapa Milk Powder Factory, Te Rapa
Raglan, popular beach, 48 km west
Waitomo Caves, 77 km south
Ruakura Agricultural Research Centre, beyond Claudelands

Cambridge

The Cambridge Museum and Te Koutu Domain and lake worth visiting. Nearby are the Karapiro hydro-electric power station, Karapiro Domain and Lookout and Mangakawa Scenic Reserve.

Huntly

Important coal mining centre with interesting opencast mine just north of the town. Nearby is Te Kauwhata, centre of viticultural research.

Matamata

Servicing area for surrounding farmland. In the area are the Matamata Hot Springs, Firth Tower, Clydesdale Museum and Kaimai Lookout.

Meremere

Home of the only coal-fired power station in New Zealand. Remains of redoubt earthworks found south of the power station. Nearby is the settlement of Mercer.

Ngaruawahia

Residence of the Maori Queen is at the Turangawaewae Pa. Pleasant picnic spot at the Point and nearby at Mt Taupiri is a sacred burial ground. A walking track runs along the summit ridge of the Hakarimata Range to the west of the town.

Okoroire

Popular resort with hot mineral baths. Good trout fishing in the Waihou River and Waimakariri Stream.

Pirongia Forest Park

Covers nearly 13000 hectares of bush dominated by Mt Pirongia and The Cone.

Pukekohe

Vegetable growing area. Points of interest include the Pioneer Memorial Cottage, lookout on Pukekohe Hill, Martyn Home at Roulston Park, Grand Prix circuit and Glenbrook Vintage Steam Railway. Nearby are evidence of an early pa site at Pukekiwiriki on Red Hill, St Bride's Anglican Church at Mauku, Alexandra Redoubt, Tuakau, fishing and holiday settlement at Port Waikato and steel mill at Glenbrook.

Te Aroha

Farming town with hot springs well known for their curative powers. New Zealand's oldest organ, the Snetzler, is in St Mark's Church.

Te Awamutu

Points of interest include St John's Anglican Church, the Gavin Gifford Memorial Museum and War Memorial Park. Nearby is the Orakau Pa, Ngaroto Lake and settlement of Pirongia flanked by Mt Pirongia, now a forest park and an area rich in Maori history.

Tokoroa

Administration centre for the afforestation area. Kinleith Pulp and Paper Mill is 6 km south of the town.

COROMANDEL PENINSULA

Coromandel

The Coromandel School of Mines Museum and camping area at Long Bay are both worth visiting. North from Coromandel are the former kauri milling centre of Colville, camping spot at Kennedys Bay, Mt Moehau, holiday sites at Port Charles and Port Jackson and mine-shaft-pocked Tokatea Hill.

Hot Water Beach

Between low and mid tide hot pools can be scooped out in the sand, at the mouth of the Tuwaiwe Stream.

Paeroa

Best known for its mineral drinking waters marketed under the name 'Lemon and Paeroa'. Primrose Hill is a good view point and old gold settlements east of the town include Makaytown, Karangahake, Waikino and Waitawheta.

Tairua

Holiday town with good bathing on ocean beach. Nearby is the seaside development of Pauanui and off shore is Slipper Island.

Thames

Gold mining relics are found at the Thames

School of Mines, Gold Battery, Queen of Beauty Pump, and Shotover Claim. Other points of interest include the Totara Pa and lookout at World War I Memorial. Nearby are the Hauraki Hot Springs and Coromandel Forest Park.

Thames Coast

Incorporates many pleasant beaches, offshore fishing, and launching ramps at Ngarimu Bay, Te Puru, Waiomu, Raumahunga Bay, Tapu and Tararu.

Waihi

Points of interest include the Catholic Church of St Werenfried, Te Heuheu Mausoleum, the Tapeka and Te Mahau carved meeting houses, the Waihi Falls, Museum and Art Gallery in Kenny St and the Martha Lake wildlife sanctuary. Just out of the town is the resort of Waihi Beach.

Whangamata

Surfing resort and holiday town. Nearby are picnic spots in the Wentworth Valley, ocean beach at Opoutere and surfcasting beach at Whiritoa.

Whitianga

Big game fishing centre with places of interest including sandy Buffalo Beach, Cooks Beach, the Ferry Landing and Shakespeare Cliffs. Nearby is a popular surfing beach at Simpsons, holiday spot at Hahei, and Cathedral Cove Recreation Centre north of Hahei.

BAY OF PLENTY

Cape Runaway

Good fishing, swimming and picnicking at Waihau Bay, Oruaiti Beach and Whanarua Beach.

Maketu

Once a thriving Maori centre and today a small settlement with interesting features such as the Arawa Canoe memorial, Te Awhi-o-te-rangi meeting house, Whakaue meeting house, St Thomas' Church and Maketu Natural Thermal swimming pool.

Mataatua

Of interest is the magnificent Te Whai-a-te-Motu meeting house. Nearby is Ruatahuna, home of the Tuhoe tribe (the 'Children of the Mist').

Matahina

Largest earth dam in the North Island, 32 km south-west of Whakatane.

Mt Maunganui

Popular surf beach and port of Tauranga. Points of interest include the Mount (an old pa site with extensive views of the area), Ocean Beach, Marineland, the Blowhole and Domain hot saltwater pool.

Opotiki

Centre of dairy and sheep farming district. Good surf beaches nearby at Ohiwa and Waiotahi. Church of St Stephen the Martyr worth visiting as is the Hukutaia Domain west of the town.

Scenic highlights in the Bay of Plenty

Native bush reserve at Hukutaia Domain
Natural forest and river scenery at Waioeka Gorge
Wild and rugged scenery at Motu Gorge, Motu Hills and Motu Falls
Trout fishing at Lake Waikaremoana
Sheer cliff at Waihirere Bluff

Tauranga

Places of interest include the Monmouth Redoubt, Tauranga Mission House, Otemataha Pa Military Cemetery, Gate Pa, Tauranga District Museum, Pioneer Village and Memorial Park. Nearby are the Katikati hot springs, Kaiate Falls, Omanawa Falls, Whakamarama Scenic Reserve and magnificent Ocean Beach.

Te Kaha

Old whaling settlement. Of interest are the Tu Kaihi meeting house, remains of an old redoubt and pa.

Urewera National Park

Third largest park in New Zealand (over 200 000 hectares) and contains a large area of untouched forest. Encompasses Lakes Waikaremoana and Waikareiti and numerous rivers; some of the finest waters for rainbow trout in New Zealand.

Whakatane

Places of interest include Pohaturoa Rock (Sentinel Rock), Puketapu Lookout, Toi's Pa, Whakatane Heads, Wairere Waterfall, Whakatane Museum and Whakatane Board Mills (cardboard production). In the area are Ohope Beach, Awakeri Hot Springs, Rangitaiki Plains Dairy Factory, the Matahina Power Station and the Urewera National Park.

ROTORUA AND THE VOLCANIC PLATEAU

Rotorua

Thermal areas at Whakarewarewa, Waiotapu, Waimangu, and Tikitere
Trout springs at Fairy Springs, Rainbow Springs Park, Paradise Valley Springs and Taniwha Springs
Other places of interest include:
Government Gardens, Arawa St
Polynesian Pools, Hinemoa St
Agrodome, Riversdale Park
Ohinemutu Maori Village
Kuirau Domain, by Ranolf St
Mokoia Island, in Lake Rotorua
Lakes Rotorua, Rotoiti, Okataina and Tarawera
Hongi's Track, on the road to Whakatane
Te Wairoa Buried Village
Blue and Green Lakes
Mt Ngongotaha
Hamurana Springs
Okere Falls
Te Amorangi Trust Museum, Holdens Bay
Waipa Mill, in Whakarewarewa State Forest
Redwood Memorial Grove
Hinemoa Point

Taupo

Lake Taupo, excellent trout fishing
De Brett Thermal Pools, on Taupo-Napier Road
A. C. Baths, Main St
Tokaanu Pool, Tokaanu
Redoubt and Old Courthouse, off Story Place
Waipahihi Botanical Reserve, end of Shepherd St

Around the lake are:
Waitahanui, fishing resort of world renown
Hatepe fishing settlement
Turangi, hydro town for the Tongariro Power Scheme
Tokaanu, hot springs
Waihi, privately owned village with hot springs
Kuratau Hydro Electric Power Station
Karangahape Cliffs
Kinloch, recent lake-side settlement
Acacia Bay, holiday homes and boats for hire
In the Taupo district are:
The Opepe Graves
Wairakei, geo-thermal power centre
Huka Falls
Aratiatia Rapids
Orakei Korako, varied thermal area
Mt Tauhara, extinct volcano and trig station
Golden Springs, warm springs with tame carp
Other places of scenic interest include:
The Tongariro River, world-famous for its fishing
Mt Pihanga, beautiful wooded slopes
Lake Rotopounamu, native bush
Lake Rotoaira, at the foot of Mt Pihanga

Tongariro National Park
New Zealand's first national park covering 75 227 hectares and dominated by the magnificent volcanoes of Ruapehu, Ngauruhoe and Tongariro. Ruapehu is extremely popular for skiing, there are hot springs at Ketetahi and the entire area is a naturalist's and hiker's paradise.

EAST COAST

Gisborne
Kaiti Hill Lookout
Cook Memorial Observatory, Kaiti Hill
Poho-o-rawiri meeting house, foot of Kaiti Hill
Cook Memorial, Kaiti Beach Rd
Statue of Young Nick, Churchill Park
'Star of Canada' house, cnr Childers Rd and Cobden St
Botanic Gardens, off Roebuck and Aberdeen Rds
Museum and Art Gallery, Stout St
Waikanae Beach
Public Library, Peel St
Wyllie Historic Cottage, Kelvin Park

Environs
Wine Museum, Waihirere
Matawhero Presbyterian Church, 7 km west
Te Hau-ki-Turanga meeting house, Manutuke
Rongopai meeting house, north of Patutahi
Gray's Hill Lookout
Wainui, Makarori and Tatapouri beaches
Rere Falls
Morere hot springs
Whitiereia meeting house, Whangara Beach

Doneraille Park
Native bush reserve and picnic spot on the banks of the Hangaroa River.

East Coast Scenic highlights include:
Te Reinga Falls at the confluence of the Ruakituri and Hangaroa Rivers
Waterfalls, fishing and bush surrounds of the Rua River
Spectacular scenery on the Mahia Peninsula
Natural forest and scenery at Waioeka Gorge
Lake Waikareiti

Hicks Bay
Camping, fishing and bathing. Tuwhakairiora meeting house is one of the finest on the East Cape. Derelict freezing works attest to the town's early commercialism.

Ruatoria
Centre of the fertile Waiapu Valley. The Whakarua Memorial Hall is worth visiting. Nearby are Mt Hikurangi (the highest non-volcanic peak on the North Island) the Ngata homestead, Porourangi meeting house and Mangahanea marae.

Te Araroa
Home of the world's most easterly hotel and a pohutukawa tree which is one of the largest in New Zealand. The East Cape lighthouse is 20 km east of the town.

Te Puia
Hot springs and picnic grounds around the small Lake Kamokamo. Nearby is the near ghost town and pretty beach of Waipiro Bay.

Tikitiki
Places of interest include the Tikitiki Mem-

orial Church and the Tawhiwhirangi marae.

Tokomaru Bay
Once centre for the freezing works industry and Mawhai Point used to be the site of a large whaling station.

Tolaga Bay
Worth visiting are Cook's Cove and The Hole in the Wall. Good swimming and canoeing area. North of Tolaga Bay are two other lovely beaches: Kaiaua and Anaura Bay.

Wairoa
Service town for the farming hinterland. Centennial Baths of good quality. Nearby is the Portland Island lighthouse, Takitimu carved meeting house, Whakaki lagoon and popular Whakamahi beach.

KING COUNTRY

Awakino
Maori cemetery here contains the supposed anchor stone of the *Tainui* canoe. Good fishing in the Awakino River.

Kawhia
Popular resort. Of interest in the town and surrounding area are the Kawhia Memorial Church, Te Puia (hot water) beach, *Tainui* canoe's resting place, fabled 'Karewa' pohutukawa tree, Arawi pa site and iron sand at Taharoa.

Ohakune
Market gardening settlement. Good fishing base and excellent scenic drive via the Ohakune Mt Rd to Mt Ruapehu.

Otorohanga
Cattle and sheep stud-breeding centre. Deer park in the town and within easy reach is the Mangapohue natural bridge and Waitomo caves with their famous glow-worm grotto.

Raurimu Spiral
Unusual piece of railroad engineering where the line runs in an ascending spiral to give a 'lift' of 150 m in a distance of less than 2.5 km.

Taumarunui
Points of interest include the locomotive 'Parliamentary Special' and canoeing down the Wanganui River from the Wanganui-Ongarue River junction. Excursions from here to Lake Taupo and the Tongariro National Park.

Te Kuiti
Headquarters of the Ngati Maniapoto tribe and site of the Te Tokanganui-a-noho carved meeting house. Nearby is the Mangaokewa Scenic Reserve and a small hydro-electric station at Piopio.

Tongaporutu
Fishing settlement with Maori rock drawings in large sea caves. South of the town is Mt Messenger offering extensive views of the area.

HAWKES BAY

Napier
Marine Parade, seaside resort atmosphere with a Marineland
The Rose Gardens, Marewa
Botanical Gardens, Hospital Hill
Nelson and McLean Parks, Napier-south
Tiffen Park, city centre
Hawkes Bay Art Gallery and Museum, Herschell St
Bluff Hill viewpoint
Waiapu Cathedral, Tennyson St
The Iron Pot inlet, Ahuriri
Holt Planetarium, Herschell St
Lilliput animated display village and model railway, cnr Marine Pde and Tennyson St
Environs
Westshore Beach, swimming and surfing, north of the city
Cape Kidnappers Gannet Sanctuary
Eskdale Park, 19 km north
Lake Tuitira, 41 km north
Waimarama Beach, 45 km south
Waipatiki Beach, 44 km north
Dartmoor picnic spot, 24 km west
Clive children's zoo, just south of Clive
Several wineries in the area

Dannevirke
Initially settled by Scandinavians. A small

deer park and aviary is found in the Dannevirke Domain.

Hastings

Places of interest include the Municipal Theatre, Library, Assembly Hall, Civic Square, Cornwall, Frimley and Windsor Parks, Oak Avenue, Maori Artifacts Room, showgrounds at Tomoana and Waikoko House. Nearby are the beach resorts of Haumoana and Te Awanga, Waimaramara Beach and Te Aute Maori boys' college.

Havelock North

Residential borough near Hastings. Worth seeing are the Te Mata Peak, Our Lady of Lourdes Church, Ashcroft's Honey House in Te Mata Rd and the Keirunga Gardens.

Manawatu Gorge

The road through this magnificent gorge was first built in 1871–2. Good canoeing in the area.

Norsewood

Scandinavian settlement. Worth visiting is the Norsewood Pioneer Museum next to the War Memorial Hall.

Waipukurau

Bustling farming centre. Places of interest include Stockade Hill, Paul Hunter Memorial Park, A'Deane Park and the Mt Herbert Reserve. Nearby are Porangahau Beach and the town of Waipawa.

TARANAKI

New Plymouth

Pukekura Park, Liardet St
Brooklands Park, Brooklands Drive
The Gables, near Brooklands Park entrance
Taranaki Museum, War Memorial Building
Richmond Cottage, cnr Brougham and Ariki Sts
Mount Moturoa lookout
St Marys Church, Vivian St
Marsland Hill, Robe St
Observatory, Marsland Hill
Govett-Brewster Art Gallery, Queen St
Bell Block Cheese Factory, Bell Block
Hurworth (house museum), Carrington Rd
Kawaroa Park, Weymouth St

Environs
Pukeiti Rhododendron Trust, 29 km from the city
Egmont National Park
Beaches at Oakura, Waitara and Opunake
Lake Mangamahoe domain, about 10 km south
Burgess Park, 6 km south

Auroa

Elysian Country Gardens are worth visiting.

Egmont National Park

Mt Egmont dominates the Taranaki landscape. There are ample climbing tracks in the park, with the main routes from the resort at Dawson Falls, East Egmont and North Egmont. It is a popular ski area in winter.

Eltham

Well known for specialty cheeses produced by the NZ Co-operative Rennet Co Ltd. Nearby is Dawson Falls, Lake Rotokare and Ratapihipihi Reserve and the Te Ngutu-o-te-manu battle site.

Hawera

Places of interest include the King Edward Park, Hicks Park, Willow Pattern Garden, Naumai Park, Turuturu-mokai Pa and Kiwi Co-operative Dairy. Nearby is Ohawe Beach.

Manaia

Farming centre with focal point of a rotunda flanked with war memorials. Has two well-preserved block houses built in 1880. Nearby popular picnic spot at Kaupokonui Beach.

Opunake

Dairy centre with good beach and sea fishing. Nearest landfall to the main offshore natural gas field.

Parihaka

Te Whiti's historical headquarters. His grave is in the centre of the village.

Patea

Formerly an important military settlement, now a market town. The Ko Rangiharura meeting house is of interest as is a concrete model of the *Aotea* canoe.

Pukearuhe

Once a block house settlement. Of interest are a cairn marking the spot where the Reverend Whitely was killed, a historic reserve and a settlers' cemetery.

Stratford

Of interest is the King Edward Park and nearby is the Stratford Mountain House and Dawson Falls. Good trout fishing in the Patea, Manganui and Te Popo Rivers. Two kilometres south is Ngaere with gardens and a pioneer village worth visiting.

Te Ngutuotemanu

Bush walks, camping and picnicking in this historic reserve where Von Tempsky died in battle.

Urenui

Birthplace of Sir Peter Buck. A striking memorial to him is found at Okoki Pa and numerous other pa sites in the area. The Mahi-tamariki meeting house is worth visiting.

Waitara

The Manukorihi meeting house contains Sir Maui Pomare's tomb.

WANGANUI

Wanganui

Queens Park, cultural centre of the city
Wanganui Public Museum, entrance from Watt St
The Sarjeant Gallery, Queens Park
War Memorial Hall, Queens Park
Cook's Gardens, heart of the city
Ward Observatory, above the Cook's Gardens
Alexander Museum and Library, Queens Park
Putiki Church, Anaua St
Putiki Pa, Kemp St
Virginia Lake, Great North Rd
Durie Hill, opposite Wanganui City Bridge
Bastia Hill Tower, Mt View Rd
James McGregor Memorial, Kowhai Park
Moutoa Gardens, Taupo Quay
Deer Park, St John's Hill
Holly Lodge Winery, Aramoho
Wanganui Woollen Mills, Aramoho

Environs
Beaches at Castlecliff, Mowhanau, Ototoka and Turakina
Bushy Park Scenic Reserve, 15 km west
Kemp's Pole, on the road to Raorikia

Rata

Noted for magnificent garden called 'The Ridges'.

Ratana

Maori township with imposing Ratana Church which houses a museum of crutches and other appliances used by the sick people whom Ratana healed.

Taihape

Old railway settlement. Places of interest include the Hautapu gorge and an interesting meeting house south of the town. Good trout fishing and hunting and jet boats on the Rangi-tikei River.

Waitotara

Small settlement rich in history of the Maori wars. The Hau haus' former stronghold was at the nearby Wereroa Pa.

Waverley

Small farming town. Of interest are the War Memorial Clock in the old Wairoa redoubt, ironsands nearby at Waipipi and unique Maori rock drawings at Kohi, about 5 km out of Waverley.

MANAWATU

Palmerston North

'The Square', commercial heart of the city
Massey University
Manawatu Museum, Church St
Rugby Museum, cnr Grey and Carroll Sts
Palmerston North Art Gallery, cnr Grey and Carroll Sts
Picnic spots on the Esplanade
Centennial Lake
Bledisloe Park
Anzac Park Lookout
Maori Battalion Memorial, Cuba St
Hopwood Clock Tower and Cenotaph, 'The Square'

Dugald McKenzie Rose Gardens
National Dahlia Trail
Environs
Tokomaru Steam Engine Museum, 19 km south
Beaches: Foxton, Himatangi and Hokoi
Picnic spots: Horseshoe Bend (Tokomaru) and Pohangia Valley Domain
Manawatu Gorge (begins 16 km out of the city on the road to Woodville)

Bulls

Small farming town on the banks of the Rangitikei River. Nearby is the Flock House Station (farming instruction), Ohakea RNZAF station, beach at Moanaroa and picnicking and trout fishing at Dudding Lake Reserve.

Fielding

Places of interest include the Fielding Sale Yards, lookout on Highfield Rd and Kowhai Park. Nearby is a picnic spot at Menzies Ford, the Mt Stewart Memorial and Mt Lees Reserve.

Foxton

Old flax and timber port. Points of interest in this area include Foxton Beach, the Moutoa floodgates, Himatangi Radio and Himatangi Beach.

Levin

Thriving farming centre with excellent recreational area at Lake Horowhenua. Also of interest are the Waiopehu Native Reserve, Ohau track climbing into Tararua Forest Park and NZ Fruitgrowers' Federation Nursery. Nearby are Waitarere and Hokio beaches, Tatum Park, Papaitonga Lake and the Levin Horticultural Research Station.

Otaki

Home of the historic Rangiatea Maori Church, one of the finest examples of Maori work in existence. Also of interest are the Otaki Maori Mission, Otaki Museum and Otaki Beach.

WAIRARAPA

Cape Palliser (road to)

Access is initially through Martinborough or Featherston. On the way, places of interest include Lake Wairarapa (yacht races), Lake Ferry (camping and fishing), the Putangirau pinnacles and Cape Palliser lighthouse. There is a small seal colony on the Cape.

Eketahuna

Scenic reserve at Makahi River Gorge. Nearby is the Mt Bruce Native Bird Reserve and railway township of Mauriceville.

Featherston

Of interest are the Fell engine (early engine designed to haul trains over the Rimutaku Ranges) and Anzac Hall. Nearby is Tauherenikau, centre for race meetings and picnics.

Forest Parks

The Wairarapa has access to the Tararua State Forest Park, the Haurangi Forest Park, and the Rimutaka Forest Park. Mt Bruce, Puketoi, Rocky Hills, Ngaumu and Tinui are also all State Forest Parks in the area.

Greytown

Oldest town in the Wairarapa. Places of interest include the Papawai marae, Soldiers Memorial Park and museum at Cobblestones (old Cobb and Co depot). Nearby is the Waiohine River Gorge.

Martinborough

Home of the Martinborough Lapidary Society and Museum. Nearby are the Blue Creek glow-worm caves and Lake Wairarapa.

Masterton

The largest town in the Wairarapa. Points of interest include Queen Elizabeth Park, Wairarapa Arts Centre, 'Golden Shears' shearing event and the War Memorial Stadium. Nearby is the Mt Bruce Native Bird Reserve, Mt Holdsworth Reserve, Tararua Forest Park and beach resorts at Castlepoint and Riversdale.

Pahiatua

Places of interest include the Carnival Park Reserve, Polish Refugees Memorial and Mangatainoka River reserve (good trout fishing in the river). The Pahiatua track leaves from here, crossing the Tararua Range to Palmerston North.

Tinui
Small township of Castlepoint Rd noted for its War Memorial Hall which displays the coats-of-arms of all the Commonwealth countries.

Turakirae Heads
Interesting 'raised beaches' formed by earthquakes. The first terrace was formed about 6500 years ago and the last in 1855.

WELLINGTON AND ENVIRONS

Parliament Buildings, cnr Lambton Quay, Bowen and Molesworth Sts
General Assembly Library, near Parliament Buildings
Katherine Mansfield Memorial, Murphy St
Old St Paul's, Mulgrave St
Government Printing Office, Aitken St
Vogel Building, Aitken St
National Museum and National Art Gallery, Buckle St
Alexander Turnbull Library, The Terrace
Otari Museum of Native Plants, Wilton Rd
Wellington Harbour Board Museum, Queens Wharf
Castle Collection of Musical Instruments, Colombo St
Tramway Museum, Queen Elizabeth Park
Botanic Gardens, Tinakori Rd
Carter Observatory, Upland Rd
Newtown Park Zoo, Manchester St
Law Courts, Ballance St
Marine Drive, 39 km skirting the harbour with excellent views of city, hills and harbour
View points: Mt Victoria, Cable Car Summit and Tinakori Hill
Beaches: Oriental, Worser and Scorching Bays, Days' Bay and Eastbourne in the east. The west coast has a number of beautiful beaches including Paekakariki, Raumati, Paraparaumu and Waikanae. Offshore is Kapiti Island (bird sanctuary).
Hutt Valley: industrial, commercial and residential area. Brown trout in Hutt River.
Akatarawa Scenic Drive: fine bush drive between Upper Hutt and Waikanae, passing Staglands Wildlife Park.
Tramping: Tararua and Orongorongo Ranges.

THE SOUTH ISLAND

NELSON

Nelson city
Nelson Provincial Museum, Isel Park, Stoke
Isel House (containing the Marsden family's collection of china and furniture), Main Rd, Stoke
Broadgreen, historic house, Nayland Rd, Stoke
Suter Art Gallery, Bridge St
South Street Galleries, South St
Nelson Harbour Board Museum, cnr Collins and Wildman Ave
Bishop's School (1844), Nile St
Nelson Library, Hardy St
Christchurch Cathedral, Trafalgar Square
Bishopdale, Waimea Rd
Parks and Reserves: Queen's Gardens, Isel Park, Botanical Reserve, Anzac Park, Pioneer Park
Princes Drive viewpoint, Princes Drive
Tahunanui, city's principal beach

Abel Tasman National Park
Trampers' and pot holers' paradise covering 18 200 hectares of bush-covered country 89 km north-west of Nelson city. Beautiful beach at Totaranui and Mt Evans at 1134 m is the highest point in the park.

Cape Farewell and Farewell Spit
The Spit is 800 m wide with sand dunes up to 30 m high. Cape Farewell and the Spit were first seen by Tasman in 1642 and the Cape is the northernmost point of the South Island. Golden Bay is partially enclosed by the Spit and Collingwood is the service town of the area. Pillar Light on Cape Farewell affords magnificent views of the area.

Cobb Power Station
Open for visitors and is reached by way of a precarious road up the narrow Cobb Valley. The station has six turbines and a capacity of 32 000 kw.

Kaiteriteri
Pretty bay with superb beach. Large motorcamp and popular with holidaymakers. At the northern end of the beach is Kaka Point Lookout, a former Maori occupation site.

211

Motueka

Tobacco, hop and fruit centre. The Te Ahurewa Maori Church is worth a visit.

Nelson Lakes National Park

Covering the south-east corner of the Nelson district and comprising 57114 hectares. Focal points are the exquisite Lakes Rotoiti and Rotoroa. The Mt Robert snowfields near St Arnaud are a popular winter attraction.

Northwest Nelson Forest Park

Includes historical Heaphy and Wangapeka Tracks and covers an area of 358841 hectares.

'Pupu Springs' (Waikoropupu Springs)

Largest in Australasia. The area was the scene of extensive gold workings. North-west of Takaka.

Riwaka

Centre for hop research. St Barnabas' Anglican Church contains quaint 1848 box pews.

Spring Grove

Birthplace of nuclear physicist, Ernest Rutherford.

Takaka Hill (Marble Mountain)

Road climbs 14 km from Riwaka to a height of 791 m then drops down to the Upper Takaka. Spectacular views over Tasman Bay and the Takaka River Valley towards the Cobb hydro station. Massive marble and granite outcrops and at the end of Canaan's Rd is the Harwood Hole, twelfth deepest chasm in the world.

MARLBOROUGH

Blenheim

Seymour Square, town centre
Blenkinsopp's Gun, cnr High and Seymour Sts
Parks and gardens: Pollard Park, Waterlea Gardens, Riverside Park, Centennial Rose Garden
Olympic Swimming Pool, near Central P. O.
Environs
Tuamarina, scene of Wairau massacre, 9.5 km north
Riverlands cob cottage, 4 km east

Brayshaw Museum Park, near Renwick Rd
Woodbourne RNZAF station, 8 km west
Renwick museum, 12 km south-west

Canvastown

Site of Wakamarina gold rush and named after the tent-dwelling population. Good trout fishing in nearby Pelorous River.

Havelock and Pelorous Sound

Havelock Museum displays items of local historical interest. Price's Gardens are worth a visit as is the quaint gabled Post Office in Main St. Nearby Cullens Point Lookout gives a spectacular view of Pelorous Sound. Launch trips leave from Havelock to visit coves and inlets of the Sounds.

Kaikoura

Third largest town of the province. The Garden of Memories nestle beneath the barely discernible traces of the Takahanga pa. New Wharf is the home of a major fishing fleet, (particularly crayfish). Kaikoura Historical Society's Museum contains Maori artefacts and whaling relics. A seal colony is at the tip of the peninsula and 2 km south of the town are limestone caves. Mangamauna Beach, 17.5 km north, is a popular surf beach.

Lake Grassmere

Pillars of salt and pink and white terraces mark the site of this well-known lake. Salt is being produced here by the solar evaporation of sea water. Nearby Cape Campbell is the most easterly point of the South Island.

Picton and Queen Charlotte Sound

Popular holiday resort. Smith Memorial Museum emphasises the whaling trade. Extensive lookouts from Victoria Domain. Star of the film *The Wackiest Ship in the Navy*, the scow *Echo* is beached opposite the marina entrance. Many guest houses are situated in secluded bays around the sounds and signs of early Maori occupation can be found at Waikawa Bay.

Port Underwood

Early scene of great whaling activity. Narrow winding road from Rarangi to Waikawa passes many fascinating points of interest and offers tremendous views.

BULLER AND WESTLAND

Greymouth
War Souvenir Museum, Tainui St
Parks and reserves: Dixon Park, King Domain, Coronation Domain, Irorangi Reserve
Shantytown, historical reproduction of an early gold-mining town, 13 km south
Wildlife Park, near Shantytown
Lake Brunner, swimming and trout fishing, 32 km south-west
Runanga, coal town, 8 km north-east
Rapahoe Beach, safe swimming, 11 km north

Arthurs Pass, Lewis Pass, Haast Pass
All give access across the Southern Alps through magnificent mountain, bush, lake and river scenery.

Charleston
An old gold town south of Westport, now almost a ghost town. Limestone caves are located nearby on the Nile River.

Franz Josef and Fox Glaciers
Internationally known glaciers. Many interesting walks in the area and ample accommodation. Lakes Matheson, Wombat and Mapourika worth a visit. Gold can still be found at Gillespies Beach near the Fox Glacier. Guided glacier trips are run regularly and ski plane flights are a highlight of a visit to the area.

Hokitika
Farming centre with gold rush history. West Coast Historical Museum contains a comprehensive collection of gold-mining equipment. St Mary's Catholic Church is the largest church on the West Coast. Mountaineering routes lead from Lake Kaniere and the Hokitika Gorge to Canterbury via the Browning and Whitcombe passes.

Okarito
Only known breeding site in New Zealand of the white heron. Many other birds congregate here during the breeding season.

Reefton
Important junction as roads from Greymouth and Westport converge here on the way to Lewis Pass. Sacred Heart and St Stephen's Churches are interesting buildings. Collection of minerals at the School of Mines. Attractions in the area include an open-cast coal mine at Garvey Creek, Black Point Museum and the ghost town of Waiuta.

Westland National Park
Extends from sea-level to a height of 3505 metres and contains magnificent attractions such as the Fox, Franz Josef and Douglas glaciers. Covers an area of 88629 hectares of mountains, snow fields, forests, lakes, waterfalls and hot springs.

Westport
Largest coal-exporting town in New Zealand. Of interest is Coaltown, a developing community project museum. Surrounding coal towns, past and present, include Waimangaroa, Denniston, Granity, Stockton and Ngakawau. Tauranga Bay is the home of a seal colony and Carters Beach a safe swimming spot. South of Westport are the blow-holes and 'pancake' shaped rocks of Punakaiki.

CANTERBURY

Christchurch
Victoria Square (Bowker Fountain and statues of Captain Cook and Queen Victoria)
Christchurch Town Hall, Victoria Square
Bridge of Remembrance, Cashel St
Canterbury Museum, Rolleston Ave
Christ's College, Rolleston Ave
Christchurch Cathedral, Cathedral Square
Ferrymead Historic Park, Bridle Path Rd
Yaldhurst Transport Museum, Yaldhurst
McDougall Art Gallery, Rolleston Ave
Canterbury Society of Arts, Gloucester St
Floral Clock, Victoria St
Riccarton House, Kahu Rd, Riccarton
Totem Pole, Harper Ave
Parks and gardens: Mona Vale, Hagley Park, Botanic Gardens, Millbrook Reserve, Queen Elizabeth II Park, Orana Park and Wildlife Reserves
Other points of interest: Avon River and Lake

213

Ellesmere; RNZAF Base at Wigram; Lincoln College; seaside settlement at New Brighton and Lyttelton Harbour

Akaroa

Historic French settlement. Places of interest include the Old French Cemetery, Church of St Patrick, Langlois-Eteveneaux House and Museum, early customs house, French Settlers' Memorial and Britomart Memorial.

Arthurs Pass

Mountain township within the Arthurs Pass National Park. Only crossing for motor traffic between the Lewis and Haast Passes. Outstanding attractions are the Devil's Punchbowl (waterfall), Mt Rolleston, the Bridal Veil Walk and Temple Basin skifield.

Ashburton

Centre of a large sheep and wheat farming area. Places of interest include Historical Society Museum, Ashburton Domain, the Town Clock, John Grogg's statue and Edward Wakefield's grave. Nearby are the small settlement of Mount Somers, Erewhon (sheep station) and the excellent fishing at Lake Heron.

Birdlings Flat

Gemstone area near Lake Ellesmere.

Craigieburn Forest Park

Lies east of the Southern Alps and within the catchment area of the Waimakariri River. Forest and tussock grasslands are set in alpine scenery.

Hanmer Springs

Thermal springs resort. Trout are caught in the Clarence, Waiau and Acheron Rivers. Conical Hill gives extensive views over the Hanmer Forest, particularly colourful in autumn.

Kaiapoi

St Bartholomew's Church and the Kaiapoi Mini Museum worth visiting. Nearby is Morwenstow Stud and Museum with collections of tack and racing paraphernalia.

Lake Coleridge

Good salmon and trout fishing and picnic area. Nearby are Lakes Ida and Lyndon, used for ice skating in winter.

Lake Sumner State Forest Park

Covers about 75 000 hectares, half of which is under forest. Lake Sumner and Lake Mason are partially bounded by the park.

Methven

Tourist centre servicing the Mt Hutt skifield and trout fishing areas on the Rakaia and Ashburton Rivers.

Mount Hutt Skifield

One of the newest skifields in New Zealand with a season lasting from about early May into October. Pleasant bushwalk nearby in McLennans Bush.

Okains Bay

Unspoilt beach on Banks Peninsula. Maori and Colonial Museum includes restored buildings. Maori Antiquities Hall houses an extensive display of artefacts.

Rakaia Gorge

Scenic area with pleasant camping and picnicking spots near the arched river bridge. A museum is at Rakaia.

Rangiora

Points of interest include the Red Lion Hotel, the Anglican Church of St John the Baptist and the Rangiora and Districts Historical Museum.

Waiau

The Cobb Cottage Museum and Waiau Presbyterian Church are of interest.

Waikari

Places of interest close to this small township include Pyramid Valley where moa bones were found, the Timpendean rock shelter with famous examples of early Maori rock art and the Waipara County Historical Museum.

Timaru

Caroline Bay, safe beach and Christmas carnival centre

Pioneer Hall Museum, Perth St

Aigantighe Art Gallery, Wai-iti Rd

Botanical Gardens, Queen St

St Mary's Anglican Church, Perth St

Catholic Basilica, Craigie Ave

Hadlow Game Park, Hadlow Rd

Museum of Childhood, near Mt Junction turn-off, north of Timaru

Maori rock drawings at Craigmore shelters and Frenchmans Gully

Railway museum at Pleasant Pt, 19 km north-west

Rhodes Cottage, the Levels, 10 km north-west

Cave

St Davids Pioneer Memorial Church is an interesting structure built of unhewn glacial boulders.

Fairlie

The seat of the MacKenzie County. A collection of relics is housed in the Fairlie Historical Museum and the MacKenzie Carnival Society Transport Museum is of interest. Just out of Fairlie is the Strathaven Clydesdale Stud, Fox's Peak skifields and the Pioneer Park picnic area.

Geraldine

Of interest are the Church of Immaculate Conception, Vintage Car Museum, Cottage Art Gallery, Waitui homestead, Linen Flax Factory and the Downs. Barkers Wines, just out of Geraldine, are the only wine cellars in New Zealand making elderberry wine. Excellent picnic places at Waihi Gorge and Te Moana Gorge. The Kakahu lime kiln, 18 km out of Geraldine, has been restored by the Historic Places Trust.

Lake Pukaki

Impressive views of Mt Cook can be obtained from here.

Lake Tekapo

Scenic lake with nearby attractions including the Round Hill skifield, a bronze monument of the collie dog, the MacKenzie Pass, the Church of the Good Shepherd and the observatory on the summit of Mt John.

Mt Cook

The highest mountain in New Zealand. Ball Hut area is the main skiing centre and the area is suitable for mountaineering, skiiing and bush walking.

Mt Cook National Park

Dominated by Mt Cook, the 70013-hectare park also contains five of New Zealand's largest glaciers and more than 140 peaks over 2134 metres. Places of particular interest are Mt Sefton, Copland Pass, the Footstool, Mt Sealy, Mt La Perouse, Dampier, the Hermitage, Glacier Dome and the famous Hochstetter Icefall.

Peel Forest

Scenic reserve and camping and fishing area. Nearby is the Mt Peel Homestead and the Mesopotamia Station, basis for Samuel Butler's book *Erewhon*.

Temuka

Places of interest include St Peter's Anglican Church, Temuka Potteries and the Domain. Nearby is a picnic area at Hanging Rock Bridge and the Arowhenua Ratana Memorial. Trout and salmon can be caught in the Opihi and Rangitata Rivers and there are Maori rock drawings at Opihi.

Twizel

Hydro town. Twizel Inn has a signboard depicting McKenzie the sheep rustler.

Waimate

Places of interest include The Cuddy (an old cottage), St Augustine's Anglican Church, Waimate Historical Society Museum, Seddon Square and Knottingly Park. Nearby is Centrewood Park and the Lower Hook Beach Monument. Scenic drives can be made to Kelcey's Bush, Hook Bush and Otaio Gorge.

OTAGO

Dunedin

The Octagon, garden area containing Robert

215

Burns statue and the Star fountain
St Pauls Anglican Cathedral, Stuart Street
First Church, Moray Place
Railway Station, Anzac Ave
Queen's Gardens, Rattray St
Cargill Monument, High St
Dunedin Public Library, Moray Place
Otago Museum, Great King St
Early Settlers' Association Museum and Portrait
    Gallery, Lower High St
Olveston, Jacobean-styled home, Royal Tce
Dunedin Public Art Gallery, Logan Park
Ocean Beach Railway (museum), Kettle Park
Cable House, Cumberland St
The Globe Theatre, London St
Burns Hall, Burlington St
University of Otago, Castle St
Knox Church, George St
St Joseph's Cathedral, Rattray St
Mt Cargill Lookout
Botanic Gardens, Great King St
St Kilda and St Clair ocean beaches
On the Otago Peninsula places of interest include:
Glenfalloch Woodland Gardens
Quarantine Island
Portobello Marine Laboratory and Aquarium
Otakau Maori Church
Pompallier Memorial
Royal albatross colony at Taiaroa Head
The Chasm and Lovers' Leap
Larnach's Castle

Alexandra

An old gold mining town with an excellent historic museum — the Sir William Bodkin Museum. Tucker Hill Lookout gives a panorama of the area. Also of interest are Shaky Bridge, the illuminated hillside clock and the picturesque boat harbour. Lake Roxburgh is a good boating area. Historic sheep stations nearby at Moutere Station and Galloway Station. Old gold towns in the area include Clyde, Matakanui, St Bathans, Hills Creek, Ophir and Oturehua (also a popular winter sports locality).

Arrowtown

Gold mining settlement. Worth visiting are the Lakes District Centennial Museum, Arrowtown Gaol, the Miner's Monument, Memorial Hill viewpoint and traces of an old gold town at Macetown. Autumn colours of the giant deciduous trees are another feature of this picturesque town.

Balclutha

Principal centre of south Otago on the banks of the Clutha River. Places of interest in the area include Lovells Flat Sod Cottages and the chicory kiln at the tip of Inchclutha. Drives can be made from here to Kaka Point, Port Molyneux Cemetery and the Nuggets lighthouse.

Catlins and Catlins Forest Park

Headquarters of the 57 000-hectare park is in Owaka. Things to see and do in the Catlins district are the Catlins Historical Society Museum, swimming and fishing at Pounawea, unspoilt beaches at Tautuku and Jacks Bay, the Jacks Bay blow-hole, camping at Purakaunui Bay, the Purakaunui Falls, Cathedral Caves, unique plant life at Lake Wilkie and pretty beach at Cannibal Bay.

Coronet Peak

Best skiing in Australasia with a long winter season. Accessible from Queenstown and ample accommodation and facilities.

Duntroon

Points of interest include the Takiroa rock drawings and St Martin's Anglican Church.

Frankton

In the vicinity are the Zoological Gardens, the lake outlet where lake Wakatipu spills out as the Kawarau River, the Kawarau Falls Homestead and Deer Park Heights (wildlife in a natural setting).

Lawrence

Oldest of the Otago gold rush towns. Short round trip through Gabriel's Gully encompasses the Lawrence flourmill site, Blue Spur Treasure House, Pick and Shovel Monument, Jacob's Ladder and Blue Spur town site. Nearby is the Victoria Dam.

Moeraki Boulders

Geological curiosity on a beach 1.5 km north of the Moeraki turn-off.

Naseby

Picturesque goldfield settlement. Places to visit include the Maniototo Early Settlers Museum, Watchmaker's Shop, Ancient Briton Hotel, Athenaeum, Welcome Inn walking track, the swimming dam above the township and the Hogburn sludge channel. Nearby are the inhospitable Kyeburn Diggings and a historic hotel at Dansey Pass.

Oamaru

Of interest are the Brydone and Northern Hotels, Gaol Stables, North Otago Museum, St Patrick's Basilica, Scott Memorial Oak and geological reserves at Target Gully Shell Pit and Hutchinsons Quarry.

Palmerston

Used to be the main entrance to the goldfields on Central Otago. Nearby are Shag Point, moa hunter camp site at Shag River Mouth and good picnic spots in the native bush at Trotters Gorge.

Queenstown

Most popular resort in the South Island, situated on the shores of Lake Wakatipu. In the town the old stone library, Government Tourist Gardens, Rees Memorial Plaque, Eichardt's Tavern, the cemetery, Queenstown Motor Museum and Bob's Peak Cableway are of interest. Tramping trips can be made to the Routeburn Valley, Dart and Rees Valleys, Rere Lake, Greenstone Valley and the Remarkables. Boat trips are made on Lake Wakatipu.

Roxburgh

Places of interest include Chinaman's Rock, Teviot Union Church, Roxburgh Museum and Roxburgh Cemetery. Nearby is the Roxburgh hydro-electric power station, the stone ruins of the Teviot Woolshed and picnic spots at Pinders Pond.

Skippers

The trip up the Shotover River Rd to the famous gold diggings at Skippers is a popular excursion. The road passes through many points of interest such as the Gates of Hell, Foots Bend and over Pinchers Bluff.

Wanaka

Township of incomparable alpine beauty. Viewpoints are the Lookout (Chalmers St), Mt Iron, Mt Roy, and Mt Criffel. Of interest is the trout hatchery, Criffel Game Park and the Maze. Glendhu Bay on Lake Wanaka looks north across the water to the Alps and is a favourite camping site. Popular tramp in the area is to Cascade River. Various cruises can be made from Wanaka.

FIORDLAND

Caples Track

Follows the Caples River and is reached by crossing the McKellar saddle north of Lake McKellar.

Eglington Valley

Fine scenic attraction encompassing Lake Gunn and Lake Fergus, camping sites at Bluffs, Knobbs Flat and Cascade Creek.

Fiordland National Park

The largest National Park in New Zealand covering 1 212 000 hectares. Contains some of New Zealand's most impressive scenery such as Lakes Manapouri and Te Anau, Milford Sound, the Murchison and Darran mountains. Several kinds of flightless birds are found in the park.

Hollyford Valley Track

Begins at Cascade Creek in the Eglington Valley, runs down the Hollyford Valley and over the Homer Saddle and back to the Hollyford River. Four or five days' duration.

Lake Manapouri and Doubtful Sound

A trip runs across the beautiful lake to West Arm, site of a unique and huge power station. From here, a bus goes over Wilmot Pass to reach the coast at Deep Cove on Doubtful Sound. Another unforgettable trip begins at Pearl Harbour, passes the Channel Islands, Hope Arm and Pomona Island and reaches the mouth of the Spey River.

Lake Te Anau

The South Island's largest lake. In the area are the Te Ana-au Caves, Fiordland National Park Headquarters, swimming and water skiing at

Blue Gum Point, and deer, chamois and thar at Wapiti Park. The Murchison Mountains lie along the western shores of the lake.

Marian

Situated at the foot of Mt Christina. Was once the site of a Public Works Depot.

Milford Sound

Notable sights are Mitre Peak, the Bowen and Stirling Falls, Anita Bay, the lookout behind the luxurious hotel. Milford Track, 'the finest walk in the world', takes the energetic traveller from the head of Lake Te Anau to Milford via the MacKinnon Pass, past the ribbon-like Sutherland Falls.

Routeburn and Greenstone Tracks

Begin on the Milford to Te Anau Road and lead through to Lake Wakatipu.

Te Anau to Milford Road

This 119-km stretch of road passes many points of interest including the Mirror Lakes, Cascade Creek, Lake Dunn, the Divide, an interesting museum at Hollyford Camp, Humboldt Falls, Homer Tunnel and the Chasm.

SOUTHLAND AND STEWART ISLAND

Invercargill

Southland Centennial Museum and Art Gallery, Gala St
Queens Park, entrance from Queens Drive
St John's Anglican Church, Tay St
First Church, Tay St
St Mary's Basilica, Tyne St
City Art Gallery, Anderson Park
Waihopai Scenic Reserve, near city's northern boundary
Seaward Bush, south-east of city
Oreti Beach, at mouth of Oreti River

Bluff

Chief port of Southland. The country's only aluminium smelter is on Tiwai Point. View from Bluff Hill is spectacular and Dog Island can be seen from here and the Stirling Point Lookout. The hulk of a whale-chaser lies on Tikore Island. The Glory Walk around the Bluff Hill scenic reserve is a pleasant tramp.

Curio Bay

Remains of a petrified forest dating back about 160 million years can be seen at low tide.

Gore

Of interest are the Remarkable Gap, Creamoata Mills, Church of the Blessed Sacrament, deer park and the gardens of the Gore racecourse. Nearby are the Hokonui Hills, Dolamore Park, Grants Bush and old gold towns of Waikaka and Waikaia.

Lumsden

Home of the 'Kingston Flyer' and base for the many trout fishing streams in the area. Nearby are the attractive Mavora Lakes and West Dome Deer Ranch (Mossburn).

Mataura

An industrial area with massive freezing works and New Zealand's largest paper mill. Good fishing in the area. Three kilometres south is the Tuturua reserve. Mataura Falls worth a visit.

Riverton

The oldest settlement in Southland and Otago. Of interest are the Riverton Museum, Howell Memorial, and Observation Point. Nearby are the Riverton Rocks, attractive beach at Colac Bay and off shore is Centre Island lighthouse.

Stewart Island

Tiny settlement at Oban where places of interest include the Rakiura Museum, Wohlers grave and memorial at Ringaringa Beach. Walks from Oban lead to Observation Rock and Mt Angelm which offers a superb view. Golden Bay is a pretty beach.

Tuatapere

Principal timber milling centre on the banks of the Waiau River. Of interest nearby are Port Craig, Preservation Inlet, Fiordland National Park, beautiful Lake Hauroko and interesting limestone area at Clifden.

Waikawa

Old whaling settlement now noted for good trout fishing. Nearby are the Niagara Falls, Chasland scenic reserve and Cathedral Caves.

Winton

Farming centre with excellent picnic places in the vicinity at Tussock Creek and Lochiel in the Forest Hill Scenic Reserve. Fishing and river swimming at Taringatura and Otapiri Gorge.

Index